Making Instruction Work

or *Skillbloomers*

*A step-by-step guide
to designing and developing
instruction that works*

Second Edition

Robert F. Mager

Books by Robert F. Mager

Preparing Instructional Objectives, *Third Edition**

Measuring Instructional Results, *Third Edition**

Analyzing Performance Problems, *Third Edition**
(with Peter Pipe)

Goal Analysis, *Third Edition**

How to Turn Learners On . . . without turning them off, *Third Edition**

Making Instruction Work, *Second Edition**

Developing Vocational Instruction (with Kenneth Beach)

Troubleshooting the Troubleshooting Course

The How to Write a Book Book

What Every Manager Should Know About Training

* Sold as a six-volume set (The Mager Six-Pack)

WORKSHOPS BY ROBERT F. MAGER

Criterion-Referenced Instruction (with Peter Pipe)

Instructional Module Development

The Training Manager Workshop

For more information, contact:
The Center for Effective Performance, Inc.
4250 Perimeter Park South, Suite 131
Atlanta, GA 30341
(770) 458-4080 or (800) 558-4237

ISBN 1-879-618-02-8 (PREVIOUSLY ISBN 1-56103-467-3)
ISBN 1-879-618-15-X (SIX-VOLUME SET)
Library of Congress Catalog Card Number: 96-72447
Printed in the United States of America

05 04 03 02 01 00 99 98 97   10 9 8 7 6 5 4 3 2 1

Contents

Kneedimples (A Magerfable)

Kneedimples

(A Magerfable)

Once upon a time in the land of Upsyde Downs, the Keeper of the Wisdom said to the next in line, "Doodly, you are soon to become of age, so it is time for you to enter the world and learn to Trip the Light Fantastic. It is time for you to become the best that you can."

So Doodly hurried off with his heart in his hand and a spring in his step, for he was truly eager to become all that he could.

When he finally arrived at what he believed to be the Greatest Learnatorium in all of Upsyde Downs, he was ushered to an audience with the Keeper of the Knowing.

"You have truly come to the right place," intoned the Keeper. "We have all of the Knowing there is to Know. So if you will learn what you are told, you will surely become all that you can."

Doodly was mightily impressed. He was sure he had found the Right Place. After all, didn't they have Starbright Projectors and Redeye Comblabulators with shimmering screens? Of course they did! Weren't the instructors the greatest stars of the Light Fantastic? Of course, they were! So, convinced of the soundness of his choice, Doodly applied himself in earnest. He listened keenly and wrote down what he heard. He put a mark beside all the right answers and wrote the most masterly essays. Inevitably, he rose to the top of the class, because there simply wasn't anything about Tripping the Light Fantastic that Doodly couldn't tell you about.

Finally the appointed day burst over the horizon. Doodly was handed his three-dimensional holographic diploma, along with as much pomp as could be arranged under the circumstances. He was so proud that he showed it to everyone in sight. But when at last the oohs and aahs abated, he tucked his diploma under his arm and went off to find . . . a Position. Naturally, he went first to Upsyde Fantasies, the most magnificent theater in all of Downs.

"Here is my diploma," he said proudly to the Keeper of the Entertainment. "I am ready to Trip the Light Fantastic and show that I have become the best that I can."

"Well, well, well," said the Keeper, with a lift of his eyebrows. "Anyone with a diploma as shiny as yours certainly deserves respect. And as we happen to have an opening for tonight's performance, you're hired."

So within hours it came to pass that Doodly faced his first Opening Night. He was so excited that his synapses literally twanged in anticipation. Then, just as he was giving his shoes a final sparkle, he heard the fanfare and the great clashing of cymbals—his cue for his first Grand Entrance. And he rushed onto the Stage of Life.

But the Glorious Triumph was not to be. For hardly had he approached the center of the stage before he got all tangled up in his own feet and fell flat on his face. Kersplat!

"Oh, my," said Doodly to the sweet young partner twiddling on her toes and trying to swallow a horrendously loud giggle. "They certainly taught me the tripping part of it, but I wonder what happened to the Light Fantastic? I could do this well before I started."

And wonder he might. Because try as he did, and he *did* try, all he could ever manage was a very ungainly but hilarious squat that caused everyone to roar with laughter whenever he walked upon the stage.

And from that day on, whenever people heard that Doodly was on the program, they would come from miles and miles and miles around to watch. Oh, not to watch him Trip the Light Fantastic, of course, because he hadn't actually been taught how to *do* that. If truth be told, they came to watch Doodly squat.

And the moral of this fable is that . . .

SKILL DOES NOT BLOOM FROM WORDS ALONE.

Or, in somewhat less poetic terms, telling isn't the same as teaching. Though it is a remarkable accomplishment to have developed the skills and knowledge needed to be considered competent in one's craft, those skills are not the same as those needed for teaching that craft. Just as an ability to *make* a tuba is not the same as an ability to *play* one, an ability to *play* one is not the same as an ability to *teach* someone else to do likewise.

Therefore, those who would like to share their competence with others will take steps to learn the skills by which that end is accomplished.

Robert F. Mager

Carefree, Arizona
January 1997

Part I

What It's All About

1

What It's All About

The world of instruction has changed from the days when instruction followed the lecture-in-the-morning-lab-in-the-afternoon approach and the only tools in the instructor's tool kit were the lecture, the lab, and on-the-job training (OJT). It has changed from the days when instructors were selected because they were good at their specialty, whether or not they knew anything about communicating that specialty to others. It has changed from the days when instructors were allowed to teach as much about a subject as time would allow, regardless of the relevance of the content to the need of the individual student. It has changed from the days when those who "winged it" in the classroom were held in awe.

Now, there is a craft of instruction rich in procedures and techniques for assuring that students develop important skills, and for sending them away with a desire to apply what they have learned and an eagerness to learn more.

This book is about that craft. It isn't about all the bits and pieces of the craft. It's only about those pieces that will ensure that (a) instruction is the correct solution to a problem, (b) the objectives of the instruction are derived from demonstrated needs, (c) the substance of the instruction is adjusted to what each student needs, and (d) instructional practices contribute to, rather than detract from, student eagerness to learn more. It's about how to make instruction work as well as possible with the tools at hand. Fortunately, those tools are within the grasp of those with even the most limited instructional resources—they need no special approval or budget to make them work.

Who It's For

This book is for those vitally important people who teach in an environment where the outcomes of their instruction are of serious consequence to both student and sponsor alike—who teach, in other words, where it matters whether the instruction accomplishes its announced goals and objectives. It is for those who teach so that others may achieve intellectual and economic independence, as well as self-respect, in their own worlds.

What It's For

The purpose of this book is to describe and illustrate the key components of the instructional craft. But just as there are far more words in the English language than you will ever need or use, there is far more to know about the craft of instruction than you can, or need to, put to practical use. This book is about those practical pieces—the pieces that will make your instruction lean, on target, motivating, and effective.

Though the chapters of this book cannot send you away highly skilled in the procedures being described, they will point you to those procedures that, if applied, will increase the elegance (effectiveness and efficiency) of your efforts.

> **NOTE:** Many instructors are literally dropped into a course, given a textbook, and told to "Go teach." Though this situation may not be ideal from either an instructor's or student's point of view, it often cannot be avoided. But even though you have to "hit the ground running," you

can still apply—immediately—some of the course improvement procedures described in this book.

ANOTHER NOTE: If, at any point, you find yourself thinking that it is impossible to apply any of the techniques described in this book because you are "stuck with the 50-minute hour," or because you "just don't have the time," skip ahead to the last chapter, "Course Improvement." Read the chapter and then apply the "Course Improvement Checklist" *to the course you are teaching or are preparing to teach.*

2
The Performance World

Why Instruct?

The only justification for instruction is that one or more people cannot yet do something they need or want to be able to do. Unless these two conditions exist, there is no valid reason to instruct.

That may sound like a trivial idea, until you consider the amount of time you've spent in classes thinking or saying, "But I already *know* that," or "I don't *need* to know that." Such thoughts indicate the waste of student time and motivation, not to mention the waste of instructional resources caused by thoughtless insistence on instructional ritual when no sound reason for it exists.

The Goal

Our primary goal as instructors should be to make our students as successful as possible while at the same time imposing ourselves as little as possible on their lives. Just as the ethical physician treats only those in need of treatment, for only so long as that need lasts, our goal is to instruct as effectively as possible for only as long as the need exists; that is, until each student can perform as desired.

And because we are humane and because our job is to help people to grow, our intent *during* instruction should be not to hurt, belittle, bore, frustrate, humiliate, insult, waste the time of, or otherwise demean, our students. In other words, in addition to fulfilling our instructional mandate, our goal should be to *do no harm*. To accomplish these intents, we seek out procedures and practices that will give our students the skills they need, as well as the motivation to use them and the eagerness to learn more.

The World of Human Performance

But accomplishing these goals requires us to use more tools than are available within the confines of good instructional practices. In fact, the world of human performance is a whole lot bigger than instruction. Before venturing into specifics, therefore, I'd like to offer some perspective on this larger performance world.

Instructional Technology

When we set out to help people to do something that they cannot now do but need to do, we dip into a bag of procedures currently referred to as "instructional technology." These are the techniques and procedures by which we influence what people *can do*. When there is a skill or knowledge deficiency to be eliminated, one dips into this bag and selects one or more remedies to solve the problem.

TERMINOLOGY NOTE: Though the current rubric is "instructional technology," we're talking about the craft of instruction, about the best procedures currently available for modifying human capabilities *through instruction*. Figure 2.1 names some of these procedures.

Figure 2.1

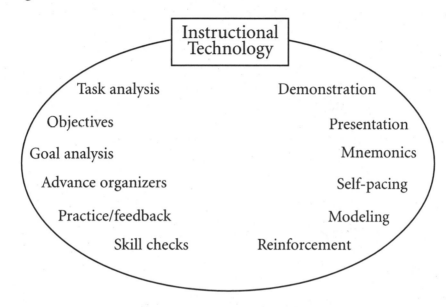

Instructional
Technology

Task analysis   Demonstration

Objectives   Presentation

Goal analysis   Mnemonics

Advance organizers   Self-pacing

Practice/feedback   Modeling

Skill checks   Reinforcement

Mission:
To change performance capability,
or what people can do.

Performance Technology

Instructional technology, however, is a subset of a larger collection of procedures and techniques known as "performance technology." When people *already know how* to perform but are not performing as desired, more instruction *won't help.* Let me say that again, and louder. ***When people already know how to perform, but are not performing as desired, more instruction won't help.*** Such situations call for application of different techniques aimed at modifying not the "can do," but the "do do" (sorry about that); techniques that encourage people to do what they already know how to do. For example, if students already know how to study but don't, more *instruction* on study skills won't help. What will help is the management of consequences that will increase the likelihood that they will do what they already know how to do.

As you are well aware, people often don't do what they know how to do, usually because of one or more of these reasons:

- They don't know what they are expected to do.

- They don't have the tools to perform as desired.

- They aren't given the authority to perform as desired.

- They're never told how well they're doing.

- They are punished for performing as desired.

In these instances, remedies other than instruction are needed; for example:

- information (manuals, policies, notices, etc.);

- authority to perform as desired;

- feedback for present performance;

- tools, space, equipment;

- performance management (arranging the environment so that desired performance is allowed and rewarded, rather than punished);

- performance (job) aids;

- task redesign (to simplify the desired performance);

- process improvement;

- interface redesign (to make the human/machine interface more logical, easier to deal with).

Some of these strategies for modifying the "do do" as well as the "can do" are identified in Figure 2.2.

Figure 2.2

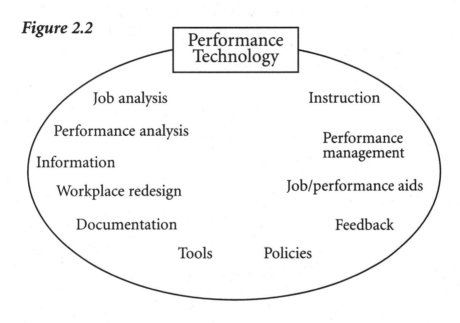

Performance Technology

Job analysis

Performance analysis

Information

Workplace redesign

Documentation

Tools

Instruction

Performance management

Job/performance aids

Feedback

Policies

Mission:
To facilitate desired performance, or what people do do.

Management

Both instructional and performance technologies are sub-sets of an even larger domain referred to as "management." Management involves the *allocation and control* of available resources toward the accomplishment of goals and objectives. That's as true of the management of a giant corporation as of the management of a ship, a church, a family, a classroom, or our own personal lives. When we are allocating and control-ling available resources to accomplish goals and objectives, we are managing. Some of the resources usually available to cor-porate managements are shown in Figure 2.3.

Figure 2.3

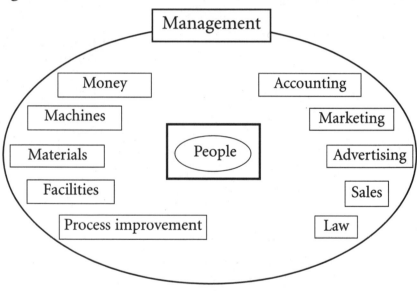

Mission:

***Allocate and control resources
to accomplish goals and objectives.***

Any corporation, for example, has a variety of resources available with which to accomplish its goals: machinery, money, production procedures, research information, marketing, advertising, law, accounting, and so on.

One of the key resources is *people.* It takes people to do many of the things that need doing. To get things done in a way that helps rather than hinders the accomplishment of the goals, however, people have to do things in a productive rather than an unproductive way. The function of the performance technology procedures is to make that happen. It reaches for the tools of that technology when people already know how to perform, and reaches for instruction when they don't.

Figure 2.4

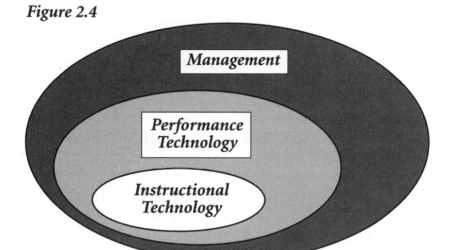

You can see by the model shown in Figure 2.4 that while instruction is an important tool for improving human performance, it is only one of the ways of doing so. For this reason we say, "We're no longer in the training business; we're in the *performance* business," and why we say, "Instruction is a last resort."

Instruction Is a Last Resort

In the past, we've been accustomed to using instruction as the remedy of choice for almost any problem involving human performance. They're not doing what they're supposed to be doing? Well, teach 'em. They don't have the right attitude, or aren't motivated? Teach 'em some more. Instruction was our magic bullet, probably because instructing was our goal. But no longer. Now *performance* is the target! The focus has changed from instruction (a process) to performance (the desired outcomes of a process). Within the instructional process itself, the focus has changed from presentations by the instructor to practice by the students.

Once the focus shifted to performance, it became clear that we already had a number of tools available to make that performance happen, and that instruction was only one of them. We also came to realize that almost every one of the non-training tools was faster and cheaper to implement than instruction. That's why we think of instruction, like surgery, as a last resort. When it's the remedy of choice, it's important that it be done— and done right the first time. But when it isn't needed, it shouldn't be done at all.

As you work through the chapters to come, therefore, remind yourself that in real life there will be many, many instances in which you won't have to complete all the steps involved in the design and development of instruction; in fact, sometimes you won't have to complete any at all. Why? Because by the time you've concluded the analysis steps, you'll have discovered how to get the performance you want or need—without the need for instruction.

To Learn More: See Resources #12 and #19. (The "Useful Resources" list can be found at the back of this book.)

3

Strategy of Instructional Development

Now that we've considered the big picture, it's time to get more specific. This chapter will present a brief description of the phases of the instructional process, as well as a description of the main techniques and procedures through which we develop instruction that works. The chapters that follow this one will describe each procedure in more detail, describe how to carry out the procedure, and offer one or more examples. Though some of the procedures may be new to you, the overall strategy will be familiar, simply because it asks you to do in your instruction what you already do in other aspects of your life: decide what you want to accomplish, apply the tools and techniques needed to accomplish it, and then determine how well you did.

The Instructional Design/Development Sequence

The procedures through which instructional design and development are carried out are often clumped into four broad phases: analysis, design/development, implementation, and evaluation/improvement. Some practitioners prefer to clump the components into five or six phases, while others prefer to think of them as fitting into three such "buckets." Don't be distressed by these preferences. After all, there are any number of ways to package a baloney; what matters is the quality of the meat. No matter which general headings are

Figure 3.1

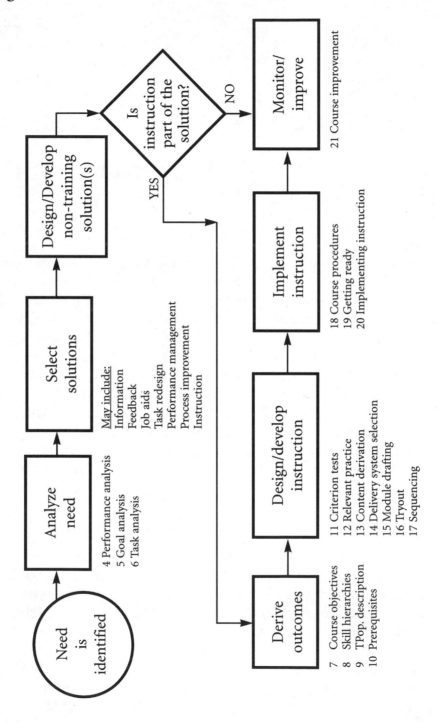

used to group the procedures, all are important to the success of the instruction.

To provide a picture of how the chapters of this book fit into the overall process, I've grouped the major steps in the process under seven general headings (See Figure 3.1). (Chapter titles and numbers are shown under the activities to which they pertain.) This diagram deliberately emphasizes the *instructional* part of the process because, after all, that's what this book is mostly about. Often, however, instruction plays only a small part in solving human performance problems. Here is a brief tour of the diagram, starting at the upper left.

Quick Tour of the Process

Analyze the need and select solutions. The process begins when a need is identified. This generally happens when someone decides that instruction is needed, or that one or more people aren't doing what they should be doing. The need is then analyzed so that appropriate actions (remedies, solutions) may be selected.

Design/develop non-training solutions. Because actions other than—or in addition to—instruction are almost always part of the solution mix, development and implementation of these non-training solutions is initiated. These remedies usually include information about performance expectancies, feedback, job aids, task simplification, and so on. (Implementation of these actions usually provides immediate benefits—whether or not instruction is ultimately included in the solution mix.)

Derive the instructional outcomes. If instruction is part of the solution, the intended outcomes (objectives) of the instruction are derived and stated, skill hierarchies depicting the relationship between those objectives are drafted, the intended student audience (target population) is described, and prerequisites are established.

Design and develop the instruction. The instruction is then designed and developed, tested, and revised, and the modules (lessons) are put into a suitable sequence for delivery to the students.

Implement the instruction. Before the course is delivered, however, course procedures are drafted so that students and instructors alike will know the rules by which the instruction will proceed. Instructors make sure they are prepared with the skills that will allow them to instruct effectively and efficiently—without detracting from the learning or from student motivation. The course is then ready for the students.

Monitor and revise. Once the course is implemented, it is periodically checked (evaluated) to make sure it still does what it was designed to do, and improvements are made where they are indicated.

That's the fast tour. Here now is a brief description of each of the chapters that follow.

NOTE: The procedures described in this book appear in the approximate order followed when a *complete* instructional development project is undertaken, that is, when all the procedures are used. But it is *not necessary to apply them in the exact order shown,* nor is it always necessary to use *all* of them to accomplish your mission.

You may want to refer to Figure 3.1 as you read the chapter descriptions that follow. Before doing that, however, read the note just above one more time.

Analyzing the Need (Part II)

The moral of one of my fables says that if you don't know where you're going, you might wind up someplace else—and not even know it. That seems pretty obvious. But how can you decide where to go in the first place? How can you decide on a worthy destination?

The analysis procedures available to the instructional developer are intended to deal precisely with these issues. They help to answer questions such as these:

- Is instruction called for in this situation?

- If not, what remedies should be applied?

- If so, what is worth teaching?

- Who is the target audience for this instruction?

- What should this instruction accomplish, i.e., what does exemplary performance look like?

The answers to these questions make it easy to prepare instruction that will teach people the things that will add value to the individual student, and to avoid teaching things that won't.

Performance Analysis (Chapter 4)

Though it often seems hard to believe, instructors are frequently asked to develop courses intended to teach people what they already know, or to use instruction to solve problems that can't be solved by instruction.

The performance analysis procedure helps to prevent these instructional errors by revealing the differences between what people are actually doing and what they should be doing, by detecting which of those differences can be eliminated by instruction, and by pointing to solutions that will help solve the problem, whether the solution is instruction or something else. This procedure is an important tool in the arsenal of those oriented toward improving performance by the best means available.

Goal Analysis (Chapter 5)

The goal analysis procedure is useful in revealing the important components of performances usually described in abstract (fuzzy) terms. Thus, a goal analysis is called for when it isn't easy to say what students should be able to do when performing competently.

If, for example, students will be expected to be "personable," or "self-starters," or "good leaders," a goal analysis will reveal exactly what a person would have to do to be worthy of that label.

Rather than be found at a particular point in the process of instructional design and development, goal analyses are completed whenever and wherever fuzzy intentions appear.

Task Analysis (Chapter 6)

The task analysis (sometimes referred to as a job/task analysis) is one which results in a step-by-step description of what a competent person does when performing a relatively sequential task, whether the steps of that task are mainly cognitive (mental) or psychomotor (physical). It is a way of making competent performance visible, much as a blueprint provides a way to make the components of a finished product visible. After a task analysis has been completed, it is possible to derive the skills that *anyone* must have before being ready to practice the entire task. In this way it is possible to make sure that all important skills and knowledge are taught.

Deriving the Outcomes (Part III)

When the analysis procedures reveal a need for instruction, the next activity is to specify the important results that the instruction will need to accomplish for it to fulfill the need. This is done by stating the instructional objectives, by depicting the prerequisite relationships between the objectives, and by determining which skills must be in place (i.e., prerequisites) before a student will be able to profit from the instruction.

Course Objectives (Chapter 7)

Instructional objectives are statements that describe the desired instructional outcomes (results); they describe what students must be able to do to be considered competent (Note: Correctly implemented instruction continues until the student can perform as the objectives describe). Objectives are derived from the skills that anyone would need before being able to practice tasks described by the analyses. They describe instructional targets, much as blueprints describe the components of a finished product.

Skill Hierarchies (Chapter 8)

Skill hierarchies are simple diagrams showing the dependency relationships between the skills that must be in place before a larger, more comprehensive, skill or task can be practiced. They are useful in determining which skills *must be learned* before others can be addressed. They also provide the substance from which course maps are derived, and with which decisions can be made about the most efficient use of limited practice materials and equipment.

Target Population Description (Chapter 9)

The target population (TPop.) description summarizes the key characteristics of those who will be the recipients (the targets, the audience) of the instruction. By knowing their characteristics, it is possible to better mold the instruction to each student: to select objectives, examples, terminology, media, and procedures that will best allow each student to accomplish his/her goals. It is one of the key techniques for making instruction work. (Note: TPop. descriptions are sometimes drafted after the instructional outcomes have been derived and stated.)

Course Prerequisites (Chapter 10)

Prerequisites describe what students must be able to do before they can profit from your instruction (they are *not* course descriptions). Prerequisites are derived from the TPop. description and from decisions about what will and will not be taught during the course.

Developing the Instruction (Part IV)

The design/development phase includes the drafting of measuring instruments (tests), as well as development, tryout, and revision of the instruction itself. Though some consider one or more of these steps to be part of the analysis phase, it is a hair unworthy of splitting.

Criterion Tests (Chapter 11)

More commonly referred to as "performance checks" or "skill checks," criterion tests are the instruments by which students and instructors can determine whether the instruction works; that is, whether a student, after instruction, can perform as an objective demands. They are the instruments by which students and instructors alike can determine whether the student is ready to move to the next unit of instruction. They are not intended to determine how well a student performed in comparison with other students, but to determine how well the student performed in comparison with the objective.

Relevant Practice (Chapter 12)

This is a description of what must be provided—the "stuff" it will take—to make it possible for students to practice the substance of the objective. The description lists tools and equipment needed as well as environmental requirements. It also lists any other *persons* that may be required for practice to occur under realistic conditions. Since practice is essential to making instruction work, it is important that the practice be crafted correctly.

Content Derivation (Chapter 13)

With objectives, criterion tests, relevant practice, and Tpop. descriptions in hand, instructional content can now be derived to facilitate accomplishment of each objective. The procedure used ensures that students will learn what they need to know, while not having to attend to irrelevant content or to study what they already know.

Delivery System Selection (Chapter 14)

This procedure determines the combination of media, resources, and other items that will be most useful in delivery of the instruction. It identifies the means by which learners will be taught what they need to know *before* they can practice, and it identifies the things that will be needed to provide the practice itself. Media decisions are made after content has been derived and are usually easy to make and take little time.

Module Drafting (Chapter 15)

Modules (lessons, instruction units) are drafted according to a "floor plan" that assures (a) practice in the objective of the module and (b) feedback regarding quality of the practice. The module also includes the knowledge that must be acquired before a student can profitably practice the objective. Performance-based rather than time-based, a module includes the instruction needed to accomplish a given objective, rather than instruction that fills a unit of time. If the previous steps have been completed (which is easier and more quickly done than it looks at this point), the instruction will practically draft itself.

Tryout (Chapter 16)

Tryouts are a key step in instructional development. They provide information about whether the instruction is working and about where improvements need to be made before they can be considered ready for delivery to the students. Those who are serious about instructional quality will always insist on at least one tryout before putting a course "on line." Instructors who must do their own development should always consider their first delivery of the course as a tryout.

Sequencing (Chapter 17)

Sequencing refers to putting the modules (instructional units, lessons) into an order that (a) maintains and enhances student motivation, (b) builds new or complex skills onto existing ones, and (c) provides periodic practice of things already learned.

Implementing the Instruction (Part V)

Delivering instruction at the state of the art means instructing in a way that will help students learn what they don't already know, as efficiently and as humanely as possible. As most instructors work under somewhat less than ideal conditions, compromises have to be made. Implementation, therefore, means instructing in a way that applies the state of the art as well as the situation will allow.

Course Procedures (Chapter 18)

Course procedures are derived from ideal characteristics and local constraints. These are written down so they may be given to the students and used as guidance by both students and instructors. A course "map" may be derived from the course procedures and the skill hierarchies; the map shows students how the course modules are related to one another and which modules must be mastered before others can be attempted, and is used to help students to decide what to do next.

Getting Ready (Chapter 19)

Before instructing, instructors need to know how to facilitate, rather than to impede, the instructional process. This includes being able to define the components of instructional success, to apply and control the favorable consequences that will be used to strengthen desired performances, to apply the modeling principles that facilitate or impede performance, and to strengthen student self-efficacy (self-judgments about the level of one's abilities).

Implementing the Instruction (Chapter 20)

The instruction is then made available to the students. For each module, students review the objective and decide whether they need instruction or practice before attempting to demonstrate their competence. If they decide they need instruction, they work through the instruction, practice until they feel ready, and then demonstrate their mastery of the objective. If they decide they don't need further instruction, they simply demonstrate their mastery of the objective. In either case, if they meet or exceed the criteria, they are encouraged to advance to the next unit. If they don't meet the criteria, the instructor (person, computer, other) diagnoses the weakness and prescribes a remedy (usually more instruction and/or more practice).

Improving the Instruction (Part VI)

Because needs and jobs change, because new technologies, materials, and devices become available, and because the characteristics of incoming students change, professional instructors take steps to keep their instruction up-to-date.

Course Improvement (Chapter 21)

Course improvement consists of, first, identifying opportunities for improvement and, second, taking the necessary steps to capitalize on the opportunities. The procedure involves comparing existing instructional practices to those that would be in effect if the instruction were functioning at the state of the art; that is, comparing *what is* with what *could be.*

Summary

- The analysis procedures will help ensure that the instruction is *worthy* of working (because it teaches the "right stuff");

- The development procedures will make sure the instruction *can* work;

- The implementation procedures will ensure that the instruction *does* work; and the

- Evaluation and improvement procedures will ensure that the instruction *continues to work* as well as possible.

What Next?

The chapters that follow describe each of the tools and procedures named above, and provide an assortment of examples. Though the descriptions are offered in the approximate order in which they are usually accomplished, it should not be implied that any step is completed and then forgotten. Instructional development always involves modification of earlier steps in light of what develops later. Further, the decision to develop instruction is discontinued whenever it is discovered that the desired performances can be achieved in other ways.

The procedures for systematic development of instruction are not limited to any subject matter, profession, or vocation. Regardless of the intent of the instruction, the procedure for its development is basically the same.

A final word before proceeding. Though the content of this book must be presented in some sort of order, you should not believe that you can reap benefits only by applying all of the techniques, and in the order presented. Your instruction can be improved by the application of almost any one of these procedures, whether or not others are applied as well. The final chapter will suggest a priority for improvement of existing instruction—a sort of "bang-for-the-buck" list that will provide clues about what might be the most productive next step.

To Learn More: See Resources #12, #15, and #19. (The "Useful Resources" list can be found at the back of this book.)

Part II

Analyzing the Need

4
Performance Analysis

Situation: *Someone has suggested that you either create a course, modify an existing course, or locate and purchase a course. You want to be sure that instruction is really needed in this situation, and if not, what else should be suggested.*

Or, you have noted that one or more people aren't doing what they're expected to do; that is, that there is a difference between their actual and desired performance. You want to know what you can do about it.

Suppose someone came to you and said, "Look. These students aren't coming to school on time. I want you to develop a course to fix that." What would you teach? The history of time? How to read clocks? The importance of promptness? Pendulum appreciation? You see the point. Students already know how to get to school on time. If they don't do it, it's because of some other reason. If there is a solution to the problem, it has to be something other than instruction.

Like a hammer, instruction is only one possible tool for getting a job done. It is usually the tool of choice when people (workers, students, managers) cannot now do something they need to be able to do. But what about those instances in which students already know how to do what they need to do? Or part of what they need to know? That is, what can you do when people can already perform as desired, but aren't doing it for reasons having nothing to do with skill? Clearly, a procedure is needed for sorting through these problems and to locate solutions that will work. Enter the performance analysis.

The performance analysis is the tool of choice when people aren't doing what they should be doing. It is a way of finding out whether the differences between what they're doing and should be doing can be eliminated by instruction, or whether some other action is called for. This procedure is especially crucial for those who are expected to develop instruction *at the request of other people*. It is needed—desperately—by all instructors who are told:

- "We need a course."

- "Improve their motivation."

- "Fix their attitude."

- "They don't understand the fundamentals."

- "We have a training problem."

Unfortunately, many administrators and managers don't yet know how to analyze problems having to do with people performance. So when they see a symptom—someone doing something they shouldn't, or not doing something they should—they jump to the conclusion that the person *doesn't know how* to do it. So they ask their trainers to provide instruction. In thousands of instances, that instruction is then used to "teach" people things they already know. A total waste. If only a small amount of time (often a few minutes will do) had been taken to find out *why* people weren't performing to expectations, a proper—and less expensive—remedy could have been selected. Hence the importance of the performance analysis.

To make sure that instruction is used only when it will teach people what they don't already know, and that solutions are found that will solve the problem, you need to begin by describing the performance discrepancy in performance terms. You need to describe:

a. what they should be doing, and

b. what they are now doing.

If a performance discrepancy exists, then you need to determine whether the difference is due to a skill deficiency or to something else. If they aren't doing what they should be doing because they don't know how, then instruction *may* be a useful remedy. But if they already know how and aren't doing it, then some other remedy needs to be applied.

With the performance analysis you will be able to:

a. identify discrepancies between what people are now doing and what they should be doing,

b. determine the causes of the discrepancies, and

c. point to remedies that will solve the problem.

Figure 4.1 Performance Analysis Flowchart

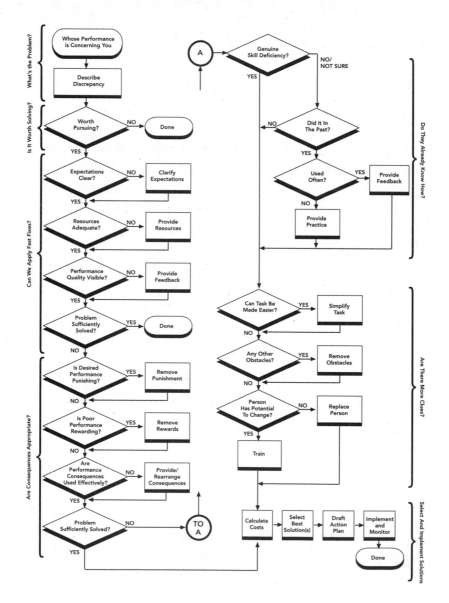

How to Do It

Here's a brief description of the steps in the procedure. Figure 4.1 offers a visual picture of the procedure in the form of a flowchart.

1. Name the category (job title) of the person or people whose performance is at issue.

2. Describe as specifically as possible what it is they *should* be doing.

3. Describe equally specifically what it is the performers *are* doing that causes someone to say there is a problem.

4. Estimate what the discrepancy is costing in aggravation, frustration, turnover, scrap, insurance rates, time lost, money lost, equipment damage, customers or good will lost, accidents, cost of a supervisor's time to fix the problem, and so on. Decide whether the discrepancy is worth doing something about.

5. If the estimated cost of the discrepancy is small, stop. In other words, if it's only a problem because you say it is, and it isn't having any impact on the rest of the world, stop.

6. Next, explore fast fixes. There are several reasons why people don't perform as expected, and some of them are so common and so easy to fix that they should be considered early in the procedure. So check to make sure that people (a) know what's expected of them, (b) have the resources (tools, equipment, supplies, etc.) needed to perform as desired, and (c) can recognize *when* they're performing to expectations. Make necessary fixes before proceeding.

7. Has the problem been sufficiently solved as a result of the previous step? If so, stop. If not, find out what happens *to the performers* when they do it right and when they do it wrong. Explore the consequences to the performers for desired and undesired performance. Answer these questions:

   a.   What happens to them when they do it right?

   b.   What happens to them when they do it wrong?

   c.   Are there any consequences at all for performing in the expected way?

   NOTE: These questions precede the next step because consequences are almost always in need of adjustment and therefore almost always suggest actions that will solve the problem without the need for more analysis.

8. If the problem is sufficiently solved as a result of adjusting consequences, test your solution(s) and devise an action plan. If not, determine whether the performance discrepancy is a genuine skill deficiency. Answer the question, "Could they do it if their very lives depended on it?" In other words, could they do it if they really had to?

9. If they could, it's not a skill deficiency, so you know that instruction will not solve the problem. You've already eliminated the high-probability causes of the problem; now you need to sort among the remaining causes.

10. Answer the question, "Did they *ever* know how to perform as expected?"

If so, and if the skill is used often, then feedback is likely to be the remedy (they aren't performing as expected because they aren't getting any information about how well they're doing).

If the skill is not used often, then review and practice, and/or provide performance (job) aids (e.g., checklists, color coding, interlocks, etc.).

11. Check whether there are obstacles getting in the way of the performer (e.g., they don't have the authority to do what's expected of them, resources aren't available when they're needed, etc.). If so, you've detected another source of the problem.

12. If you are dealing with a genuine skill deficiency, and the performers never did know how to do it in the past, then explore whether the task(s) can be simplified—made easier. This can often be accomplished by changing the task itself or by supplying checklists, procedures, diagrams, manuals, color coding, etc., to aid the performer.

13. If the problem persists, determine whether the performer has the potential to learn to perform as desired. If not, then you'll need to replace the performer with someone more likely to succeed.

14. If the performer does have the potential to learn what's needed, then consider instruction as a solution.

15. If you're doing a complete performance analysis, that is, going through all the steps without stopping to apply solutions, then you're ready to sort through the solutions and select those that will be most appropriate and cost-effective. During the analysis you will have identified

several possible causes, and now you should calculate how much it would cost to fix each of them.

16. Select the best solution(s)—those that will impact the problem, are within your power to apply, and cost less than the problem itself.

17. Draft an action plan. This simply means to say specifically who will implement each solution and how you will get them to do it.

18. Implement the solutions and check on the results.

A performance analysis usually takes less time to complete than to describe, simply because the solutions to performance problems are usually easy to spot once you begin asking the right questions. For example, why don't students ask questions when they don't understand? In many instances it's because they get punished when they do—because the instructor insults and embarrasses them in public. Why don't salespeople behave in a customer-oriented way? Because nobody has told them what that means. Why don't workers solve problems themselves, rather than asking the boss to do it? Because they haven't been given the authority to do it. And so on.

Yes, it's often that simple to solve problems of human performance. Sometimes it's a little more difficult, but usually only because information has to be collected before the analysis questions can be answered. Here's an example.

Example: In this example, an instructor who teaches computer repair in a technical school is approached by the Dean.

> *Dean:*   We need to beef up your course on trouble-shooting.

Inst: I'm certainly willing to do that. What seems to be missing?

Dean: Well, I've had calls from a couple of companies who are complaining that their troubleshooters won't use the hotline when they're supposed to.

Inst: What do you mean?

Dean: If they can't clear up a problem within 22 minutes, they're supposed to call the hotline and talk to the "hotshot" about it. But they don't do it.

Inst: What do they want me to do about it?

Dean: They think you should beef up your course.

Inst: Don't the troubleshooters know how to use the telephone?

Dean: Of course they do.

Inst: Do they know the procedure for calling the hotline?

Dean: Of course they do. But they don't use it.

Inst: So they know what's expected of them, they have the necessary tools and procedures, and they already know how to do what they're supposed to do. That tells us that instruction isn't going to help. Would it be OK for me to talk to a couple of their troubleshooters?

Dean: I don't see why not.

(Two days later.)

Inst: I think I've got a handle on this problem.

Dean: What did you find out?

Inst: Well, when troubleshooters call the hotline, they're likely to get some verbal abuse—sarcasm—from the hotshot on the other end of the line. Comments like, "What? You *still* haven't learned to solve that simple problem?"

Dean: That would hardly encourage anyone to call a second time.

Inst: There's more. If the hotline is called, and then the troubleshooter fixes the problem alone, the hotline gets credit for the fix.

Dean: Good grief.

Inst: There's even more. Troubleshooters are expected to stay on the problem until it's fixed. If they don't fix the problem by the end of the working day, they're supposed to stay with it until it is fixed. Of course, they get overtime pay for staying late.

Dean: Some system.

Inst: Yep. It's another case of performers being soundly punished for doing the very thing they're expected to do, and rewarded—with overtime pay—for doing what they aren't supposed to do.

Dean: No wonder they don't do what they're supposed to do—and know how to do. What do you suggest?

Inst: I suggest you talk with the managers who brought this up, and gently ask them the questions that will make it clear to them that company policy is getting in the way of desired performance. I'd suggest you try to lead them to see that the solution to this problem isn't instruction, but a change in the way performers are treated when they do what's expected of them.

As pointed out earlier, everyone who is concerned about the performance of others needs to be able to use the performance analysis procedure.

To Learn More: See Resources #4, #6, #7, and #17. (The "Useful Resources" list can be found at the back of this book.)

5
Goal Analysis

Situation: *While deriving the important outcomes of your instruction, you've run into some abstract expectations, such as "They should be motivated," or "They should be more safety-conscious," or "They don't have the right attitude." You want to know how to handle those abstractions and learn what, if anything, you'll need to teach to better accomplish those goals.*

Suppose that you've just completed a job analysis and shown your work to someone whose opinion you value who says, "This is great. This is just what these people are supposed to do," and then adds, "But we also want them to be conscientious about their work and more thorough in their reporting. And it's important that they be professional." Since you can't watch people conscientiousing, or thoroughing, or professionaling, what to do?

The fact is that not everything we want people to be able to do can be described in terms of tasks—not everything can be directly observed. Sometimes, rather than being expected to carry out tasks, people are expected to exhibit certain characteristics, states, or traits.

For example, you may decide, or be told, that students should:

- be motivated,

- demonstrate courtesy to _____,

- be safety-conscious,

- value total patient health,

- have good analytical ability,

- be problem-solvers,

- be self-starters,

- exhibit good leadership characteristics,

- be empowered,

or any of hundreds of other possible states. When expectations are stated as "fuzzies"—vague terms—a task analysis, which you'll read about in the next chapter, won't help. Since there is no task to watch anyone perform (you can't watch people leadershipping or attituding), a different tool is needed.

Enter the goal analysis. The purpose of the goal analysis is to determine what it would take in the way of observable human performance to be able to say that the goal had been accomplished. The purpose is to say what someone would have to do to be considered "safety-conscious" or "competent"—to say what someone would have to do to be worthy of being labeled as having achieved the goal. In other words, the goal analysis will show you how to recognize one when you see one.

When to Do It

Frankly, it would be nice never to have to do a goal analysis. But alas, people (including ourselves) don't always say what they mean. That being the case, we need to have a procedure handy (like a fire extinguisher) that we can throw into the breach when the need arises. When does the need arise? When there is an important goal to achieve that hasn't yet been described clearly enough to let you select the means of achieving it. The goal analysis procedure is used whenever you have to answer questions like these:

How can I help them to understand?

What do they mean by "fundamentals"?

How can I make them more motivated?

How can I teach them to be diligent?

What do I do about the "affective domain"?

How can I help them to be more "safety conscious"?

There isn't any one point along the development trail where you stop to do a goal analysis; you do it whenever the fuzzies creep out of the woodwork—that's when you take a little time out for some fuzzy-slaying.

© Dilbert reprinted by permission of United Feature Syndicate, Inc.

When Not to Do It

Everything called a goal is not suitable for goal analysis—only those which focus on some desired human attribute and lead to a description of *desired human performances*. Analysis of goals such as "provide good customer service," "be professional," and "speak pleasantly," deserve goal analyses because they refer to something you want people to do and because the analysis will result in a list of desired people performances. Organizational goals such as "Let's double the market share," or "We need to go global," on the other hand, refer not to people characteristics but to corporate characteristics. Goal analysis in these situations is not appropriate because the results lead not to descriptions of human performance, but rather to descriptions of organizational performance.

How to Do It

There are five steps to the procedure. The steps are repeated as needed. Here they are.

1. Write down the goal, using whatever words best express your intent. Be sure your statement is described in terms of outcomes rather than process. For example, make it say, "*Have* a favorable attitude toward _____," rather than "*Develop* a favorable attitude toward." That will help keep you out of the trap of thinking about *how* you are going to accomplish the goal before you know what the achieved goal should look like. In other words, it will help keep you from fussing around with bows and arrows before you've constructed the target.

2. Think about what would be happening if the goal were achieved. Think in terms of people performance. What would people have to do or say, or refrain from doing or saying, before you would be willing to say that they had

achieved the goal? List as many performances as you can think of. Don't edit. Just list.

3. Sort the list. Many of the items you listed will be as fuzzy as the one you started with. That's okay. Put a mark beside the fuzzies, write them on another piece of paper, and apply Steps 1 and 2 to these new fuzzies.

    Continue until you have a list of performances that collectively represent the goal. Continue until you can say, "Yes. If people did these things and refrained from doing these other things, I would say they had achieved the goal."

4. Expand the words and phrases on your list into complete sentences that tell when or how often the performance is expected to occur. This will help you to place limits around the expected performances. It will help to say "how much" performance will satisfy you (or someone else). For example, a goal analysis on security-consciousness included the item, "No unattended documents." When expanded into a complete sentence, it read, "Employee always locks sensitive documents in safe before leaving the room."

    This step will also help you to weed out statements that, on second thought, don't say what you mean.

5. Test for completeness. Review the performances on your list (there will usually be from one to seven items and only occasionally more), and ask yourself, "If someone did these things, would I be willing to say that he or she is _____ (goal) _____?" If so, you are finished with the analysis. If not, return to Step 2 and add the missing performances.

Example #1: A shop instructor I once knew completed a list of tasks he wanted his students to be able to perform when they left his course. But he was uneasy about the list.

"There's something missing," he said. "There's more to it than just these tasks."

"Oh," I said. "Can you give me an example?"

"Sure," he replied. "I want them to be safety-conscious."

"That sounds reasonable," I said. "Can you tell me how to recognize a safety-conscious person when you see one?" And we were off into a goal analysis. Not long after, we had a list of "performances" (Step 2) that included these items:

- Understands the need for safety practices.

- Wears hard hat in designated areas.

- Sweeps shavings from work area.

- Wears safety goggles while performing designated tasks.

- Uses saw guard on table saw.

- Appreciates safety equipment.

"How can you tell when someone understands the need for safety practices?" I then asked.

"Well, they follow the safety rules," was the reply. So we replaced the fuzzy with "Follows safety rules."

"How can you recognize someone who appreciates safety equipment?" I asked next.

"Easy," he said. "They take good care of it."

So we deleted that fuzzy as well and replaced it with a performance. Our list then looked like this:

- Follows safety rules.

- Wears hard hat in designated areas.

- Sweeps shavings from work area.

- Wears safety goggles while performing designated tasks.

- Uses saw guard on table saw.

- Keeps safety equipment in good working condition.

Since we could tell whether these items were or were not happening, we moved on to the fourth step. When we were done, our items looked like this:

1. Follows all posted safety rules whenever in the shop.

2. Wears hard hat each time a designated area is entered.

3. Keeps lathe area clean by sweeping shavings into the bin provided.

4. Wears safety goggles while performing the tasks posted.

5. Does not remove saw guard without permission while using table saw.

6. Keeps personal safety equipment in good working condition.

7. Reports faulty shop safety equipment.

Your definition of safety-consciousness would be different, of course, because your situation and environment are different. But that doesn't matter. What matters is that you describe what it would take for the goal to be accomplished. Only then will you know what action to take to accomplish it.

The final step was simple. When my friend said, "Yes, if people did those things on the list, I'd be willing to say they were safety-conscious," we were done with the analysis.

Example #2: While working with the training staff of an automobile manufacturer, I was told that one company goal was to improve customer service over the coming year.

> "No," the training director said after thinking about it, "that isn't quite it. What we want to do is to provide quality service."
>
> "Where?" I asked.
>
> "In auto service," was the reply.

It was important to determine just what part of the business he was talking about, because the definition of "provide quality service" would be different in the bookkeeping department (or most anywhere else) than it would in auto service.

After working through the first four steps described above, we had a list of performances that looked like this:

- Customer complaints are written down.

- Service reps refrain from arguing with customers.

- Service reps smile when talking with customers.

- Service reps listen carefully (i.e., do not have to ask customers to repeat things they have already said).

- Repaired autos are ready when promised.

- Repaired autos are returned to customers without dirt or grease, either inside or outside the car.

- Causes for the complaints have actually been remedied.

- There is less than one percent return (cars returned because the repair was not properly completed).

"If these things happened," I then asked, "would you be willing to say that you were providing quality service?"

"Well . . .," was the cautious reply, "I guess so. But we want to provide the quality service without the mechanics using up more parts than they need."

"I can understand that. But does the number of spares used have anything to do with how you would recognize quality service?"

"I guess not directly. But it's important."

"Tell you what. Let's focus on quality service until we're sure we can recognize it when we see it, and then we'll move on to the spares issue."

Which we did.

Example #3: Believe it or not, the following flowchart was developed as a result of a goal analysis. An instructor was asked to develop instruction that would teach students to use "good judgment" when deciding which criterion level to assign to each (military) task to be taught. She saw immediately that it would be impossible to decide what, if anything, to teach until she knew what "good judgment" meant in terms of human performance. After her goal analysis was completed, she saw that it would be easy to convert the results into the following flowchart. In effect, the flowchart says that performers will be using good judgment when they follow its steps.

Figure 5.1

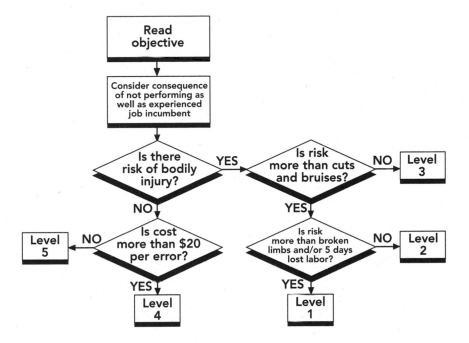

Example #4: While conducting a recent workshop in Beijing, China, one participant explained how important it was for American expatriates to have a "working knowledge" of Mandarin. "If they can't work in Mandarin," he said, "we can't hire them." Because it was unclear just what "working knowledge of Mandarin" meant, he carried out a goal analysis. Initially, his list looked like this:

- Can communicate in Mandarin.

- Can understand the Chinese.

- Can read Mandarin.

- Can write in Mandarin.

Not bad, but the list still contained four fuzzies. After further work, his description of "working knowledge of Mandarin" looked like this:

- Can express themselves verbally in Mandarin well enough to be understood by Chinese business people.

- Can repeat accurately what was said in Mandarin.

- Can read work-related reports and Chinese newspapers; i.e., can accurately describe what is read.

- Can write reports and correspondence well enough to be understood by Chinese business readers.

As you can see, the purpose of the goal analysis is to reveal the meaning of vague terms and expressions so that you can decide what to do to get more of what's wanted.

NOTE: When trying to determine the meaning of someone *else's* fuzzy, there's a right way and wrong way to go
about it. The wrong way is to ask someone to write down
what they mean by the fuzzy. This is intimidating and
threatening and won't get you very far, because they won't
know how to do what you've asked. They won't know
what they mean by their fuzzies without some serious
thought. The right way is to do it yourself. Write out what
you think the vague terms mean, and then show it to the
other person while asking, "If _____ did these
things, would that satisfy you?" It's a lot easier for people
to fix things than to create them.

Remember that when someone speaks to you in fuzzies,
they are abdicating to you the power to say what they mean.
Grab it! Say what *you* think the fuzzy should mean, and then
offer it for approval.

ANOTHER NOTE: Don't do goal analyses in a group—
it'll take forever. If you must get the agreement of others
on the meaning, work with one person at a time. Otherwise, you may be "grouped" or "teamed" to a frazzle.
Besides, working one-on-one helps spare the loss of face
when the fuzzy-utterer discovers how simply the fuzzy
can be defined.

What to Do with It

Once the goal has been analyzed into the performances that represent its meaning, it's easy to see what to do next.

1. Put a check-mark beside each of the things that students can already do. If they can already do it, you won't get more of it by "teaching" it. If they know how to do it but *aren't* doing it, complete a performance analysis to find out why they aren't doing what they know how to do.

2. Consider the items not checked. If they can't do it and need to be able to do it, you or someone else will need to teach them to do it. Decide who will teach what.

3. Complete a task analysis for each of the tasks that must be taught. (See Chapter 6, *Task Analysis.*)

4. Write objectives to describe the main outcomes you need to achieve, and then follow as many development steps as needed to facilitate the performance you need.

To Learn More: See Resources #3 and #9.

6
Task Analysis

Situation: You suspect there are things people should be doing that they cannot now do. To verify whether instruction will be needed, you want to paint a picture of what competent people do when performing the way you need others to perform.

One of our goals is to develop and deliver instruction that prepares people to perform in a useful manner in a "real world" situation, whether that "real world" happens to be a job or another course. Another goal is to make sure that the instruction itself teaches those useful skills with as little wasted motion and effort as possible. To accomplish those goals, we need to know what people have to be able to do before they can begin practicing the tasks to be performed. Enter the task analysis.

Task analysis is the name given to a collection of techniques used to help make the components of competent performance visible. It's a set of ways to draw a picture of what competent people actually do, or should do, when performing a task. From this picture it is then possible to derive the skills that anyone would have to have before they, too, can perform the task competently. It is a way to visualize the steps and decisions involved in carrying out a procedure.

There are several ways to go about a task analysis. Some of the approaches break desired performances into microscopic detail; and others, only into moderate detail. In practice, one uses the procedure that provides the level of detail needed to get the job done; that is, the level that will make the analysis serve its purpose. That means using the analysis procedure that will best answer the questions, "What do competent people do when performing this task?" and "What would *anyone* have to know before he or she could begin practicing this entire task?" The procedure described below will be useful in most of the situations you will encounter.

What's a Task?

A *task* is a series of steps leading to a meaningful outcome. There. That's the standard definition, but it's only helpful once you know what it means. Think of it this way: Every job is made up of a collection of tasks, things that you do during the course of a month that you refer to as "my job." (Note that these tasks are not necessarily related, that your job does not necessarily consist of a *coherent* set of tasks. For example, you may find yourself answering the telephone one minute, filling out a form the next, and dictating a letter the next. At home, you may find yourself making a meal one minute, rebuilding your car the next minute, and taking out the garbage the next. These are tasks that are all part of the "job," but are not related to one another.) These tasks have a beginning, a middle, and an end.

You are referring to a task whenever you ask someone to "Go and _____": take out the garbage, tie off an artery, change a tire, set a bone, interview a prospective employee, write a report, analyze a report, sell a product, make a verbal report, cut a head of hair, do a pre-flight check, adjust your computer printer driver, and so on. Each of these tasks has a beginning and an end, with a series of steps in between.

A *step* in a task, on the other hand, would be something like tighten a nut, pick up a scalpel, select a component, ask a question, press RETURN, enter name in box 3, remove the cover, or take a deep breath. Each represents *one* of the actions that need to be taken in order to accomplish the meaningful outcome. Here are some other examples of one step in each of several tasks.

Task	Step in the task
Disassemble a device	Disconnect power
Make a dress	Pin pattern to fabric
Pick a lock	Select picks
Play a part (in a play)	Speak lines
Cash a check	Verify endorsement
Apply at bank for a loan	Grovel

Who Should Do It?

Who should carry out the task analysis? That's easy. If there isn't anyone else to do it, and if it hasn't already been done, then you're elected. Fortunately, that doesn't mean you'll be saddled with an impossible or time-consuming chore. In fact, you may find it rather enjoyable. All you need to do is locate, observe, and interview a competent performer (who may be yourself).

"Wait a minnit," you may be shouting. "I can't spend time going to where people are performing the job or profession I'm teaching. Besides, I don't teach the entire curriculum. My students don't go directly to the job; they go to other courses."

Good point, and I understand your predicament. Analysts in industry have little difficulty deriving their instruction from observation of exemplary performers. Those analysts are able to observe (or study descriptions of) exemplary performance so that they can say, "Aha. *This* is what we want people to do on the job; *those* are the things they don't yet know how to do; so here are the things we will have to teach them."

Those teaching in educational institutions, however, are working in a "cottage industry" environment where instructors often behave as though they were in "business" for themselves. This is an environment where each instructor decides what to teach and how much of the subject to include in the time allotted; where five instructors teaching a course with the same name are likely to be teaching five different courses; where the objectives of one course in a series are seldom derived from the prerequisites of the next one in line; where the objectives of the last course in line are seldom derived from any aspect of the real world where the learned skills are expected to be applied.

But all is not lost. You can use yourself as one source of information for the task analysis. Then again, you must know some people who do this thing in the "real world." You can talk to them, and maybe observe them as they work. And you can find out from the instructors of the next courses in the sequence what they expect students to be able to do when they enter those courses, because their prerequisites should be, at least in part, your objectives.

How to Do It

The task analysis involves: (a) drafting a task list (an activity sometimes referred to as job analysis) and then (b) describing the steps in each of the tasks listed.

Task Listing

The first step is to list all the tasks that make up the job. It makes no difference that one task may be considered critical and another trivial. They are *all* to be listed, so that a complete snapshot of the job can be studied. If those performing the job are expected to perform a task, write it down. You will decide later which tasks will need to be learned and whether you will be the one to teach them.

For example, nearly every job involves some sort of paperwork. People are expected to complete forms, write reports, read job tickets, fill out requisitions, write letters, and so on. If paperwork is expected, those tasks should be included on your list.

Many jobs also require people to interact with other people. Sometimes it is with customers, sometimes with patients or victims, sometimes with superiors, with colleagues, or with spouses. Appliance-repair people are expected to "instruct customers" on how to avoid certain problems in the future. Managers are expected to "conduct exit interviews," and police officers are expected to "interview witnesses." Whatever its nature, if the competent job performer is expected to do it, add it to your list. Here's an example of a task list.

Example: Electronic Technician.

1. Troubleshoots to locate troubles.

2. Clears troubles from equipment.

3. Completes parts-requisition forms.

4. Reads schematic and/or wiring diagrams.

5. Uses test equipment to make measurements.

6. Calibrates test equipment.

7. Interprets test results.

8. Records test data.

9. Solders components.

10. Applies first-aid procedures.

11. Cleans and sharpens tools.

12. Cleans work area.

13. Disassembles equipment.

14. Assembles equipment.

15. Elicits symptoms from customers.

Notice that each of the items on this list begins with a verb, a "doing" word. This is one way to tell whether the item being described is a task or just a piece of subject matter. For example, if an item reads "anatomy" or "measurement," you would know instantly that subject-matter is being described rather than tasks. If a subject-matter item cannot be described in "doing" terms, it should not be included in the task list.

Task Detailing

The second step in the analysis is to list the steps and decisions involved in performing each of the tasks on the list. For each task, answer these questions:

1. When is the task performed (what triggers initiation of the task)?

2. How is the task performed (what are the steps followed and decisions made while performing the task)?

3. How would you know when you're done (when the task has been satisfactorily completed)?

There are two common ways to analyze a task, by listing and by flowcharting.

Listing. One way to make the components of a task visible is to simply list them as you would build a shopping list. Here are two examples:

Example #1: Task: Start an IV.

When initiated? When patient's chart says to do it.

1. Read patient's chart.

2. If IV is not called for, stop.

3. If IV is called for, collect equipment.

4. Get material to be administered.

5. Locate patient.

6. Verify that correct patient has been located.

7. Prepare patient psychologically for the procedure.

8. Sterilize site where needle is to be inserted.

9. Locate vein.

. . . and so on.

When completed? When IV is running according to requirements.

Example #2: Task: Clean spark plugs.

When initiated?   a. Plugs are dirty.
                      b. Customer asks.

1. Open hood.

2. Locate spark plugs.

3. Cover fender with protective material.

4. Remove ignition wires.

5. Remove plugs.

6. If plugs are cracked or worn out, replace them, and then go to Step #12. If not, go to Step #7.

7. Clean the plugs.

8. Check gap in each plug.

9. Adjust gap as necessary.

10. Test the plugs.

11. Replace plugs.

12. Re-connect ignition wires.

13. Check engine performance.

14. If OK, go to step 16.

15. If not OK, complete the designated steps.

16. Clean tools and equipment.

17. Clean any grease from car.

18. Complete required paperwork.

When is task complete? Engine runs smoothly.

Even though these examples described relatively simple tasks, you will note that it is somewhat awkward to show *in a list* the decisions to be made and just how the actions resulting from those decisions should be handled.

Flowcharting. There is a better way, called flowcharting. A flowchart is easy to read and clearly shows the alternatives to be followed when decisions are involved. Furthermore, it reveals where information is still missing.

To flowchart a task, you need only two symbols to depict the steps of the task: a rectangle to depict actions and a diamond to depict decisions (see Figure 6.1). Other shapes, such as ovals and squares, may be used to depict various outcomes, but the rectangle and the diamond are all that are needed to show the components of the task itself.

Figure 6.1

Begin by writing down the event that causes the task to be performed. Here are a few example events that initiate tasks:

- Phone rings.

- Customer asks _____.

- Red light comes on.

- Grinding sound is heard.

- Screen shows error message.

- Patient screams.

Then write down what happens next. If it's an action, write it in a rectangle. If it's a decision, write it in a diamond, and draw lines from the diamond to the different actions that would result from the decision. Sometimes there are several actions that might be taken as a result of a decision. For example, if the pressure is less than 10 lbs., do thing A; if the pressure is between 10 and 50 lbs., do thing B; if the pressure is more than 50 lbs., run! Usually, though, there are only two alternatives: Do thing A if the decision is yes, and do thing B if the answer is no. For example, if I were to flowchart the spark plug cleaning example, it would look like this:

Figure 6.2   **Clean Spark Plugs**

When initiated?   a. Plugs are dirty.
                            b. Customer asks.

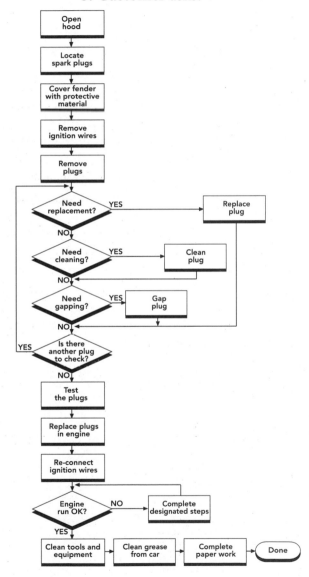

When terminated?   Engine runs smoothly.

NOTES:

a. Don't include instruction in the analysis. The purpose of the analysis is to visualize competent performance so that better decisions can be made about how to get more of it. Putting "how to learn it" comments in the task analysis puts the cart before the horse and defeats its purpose.

b. Statements such as "Select a screwdriver" or "Select a lipstick" are not considered decisions and don't belong in a diamond; no matter which screwdriver or lipstick is selected, the action that *follows* is the same. Use a decision symbol only when one decision would lead you to a different *action* than would another decision.

c. Don't be concerned if one part of your analysis seems to be more detailed than another. The purpose isn't to produce some tidy document for display; the purpose is to help answer the question, "What would *anybody* have to be able to do before practicing this entire task?" When the analysis is detailed enough to answer that question *for each* step, consider it finished.

d. The quality of the analysis is unrelated to the straightness of your lines. So don't waste time with a ruler. Do your flowcharting on a large piece of paper, and do it with a pencil. If you prefer, flowchart the task using a computer-based flowcharting-application program.

The following examples provide three additional flowcharts.

Example #1: This flowchart depicts the main actions followed by someone troubleshooting equipment at the customer's location.

Figure 6.3   **On-Site Troubleshooting**

When initiated? Malfunction report received.

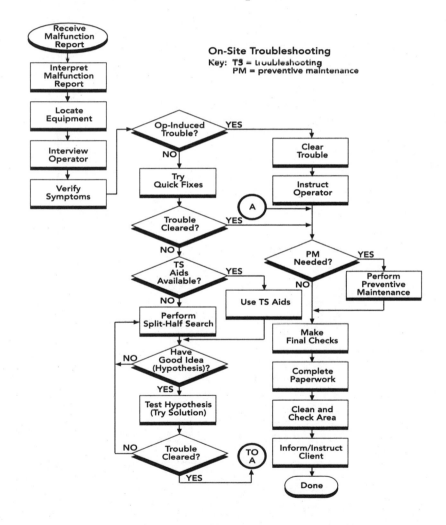

When terminated? Equipment functions according to specifications.

Example #2: This flowchart shows the steps followed when conducting a performance analysis.

Figure 6.4   **Performance Analysis**

When initiated?   Someone's performance is less than adequate.

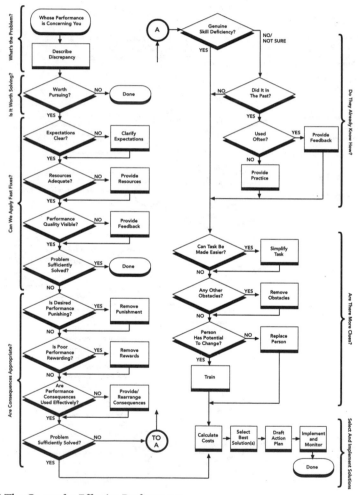

© 1997 The Center for Effective Performance

When terminated?   Cause(s) and remedies have been identified.

Example #3: Here is a flowchart showing the key steps in conducting a task analysis when the information is to be obtained from a subject-matter specialist.

Figure 6.5   **Conduct Task Analysis**

When initiated?   The details of competent task performance need to be described.

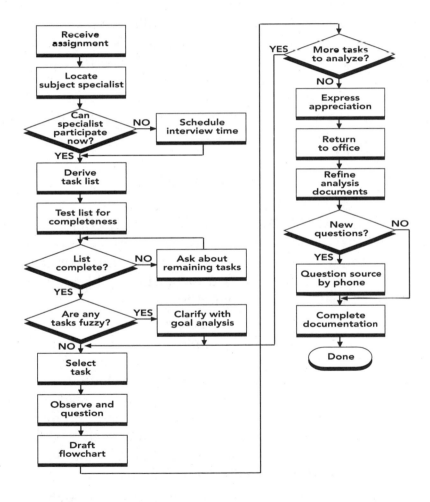

When terminated? All key actions and decisions are described in the sequence in which they are performed.

Sometimes, when products are so new that subject-matter specialists do not yet exist, the task analysis has to be done by analyzing the available documentation (e.g., engineering drawings) to answer the question, "What do we *imagine* someone will be doing when performing this task?"

Deriving Skills

Once the task analysis shows the components of competent performance, you can then derive the skills that *anyone* would need to have before practicing the entire task. To do this you need to forget about students for the moment (though you'll think a great deal about them later). At this point you are interested only in naming the skills that *anyone in the world* would have to have before practicing the task step you are considering.

How to Do It

1. Consider each step of your analysis in turn.

2. In a column to the right of the step, write the skills that anyone would have to have before they could practice that step. Note: Lots of steps won't require you to write anything beside them because they are simple or have no sub-skills, such as, "Pick up wrench," or "Locate Box 3." Don't make it harder than it is.

3. When you have finished, delete the duplications from your list of skills. For example, it is likely that you have written "Read English" beside several of the steps, because, among other things, someone would have to be able to read to perform that step. If the reading skill required for each step is the same, delete the duplications. If, however, different levels of reading skill are required for the various steps, they do not represent duplications and should not be deleted.

4. Later on, you'll draft an objective to describe each of the remaining skills.

Example #4: This example shows the skills that anyone would need to perform three of the steps in the troubleshooting task shown earlier. (Initiating and terminating cues are not shown.)

Figure 6.6 **Troubleshooting Skill Requirements**

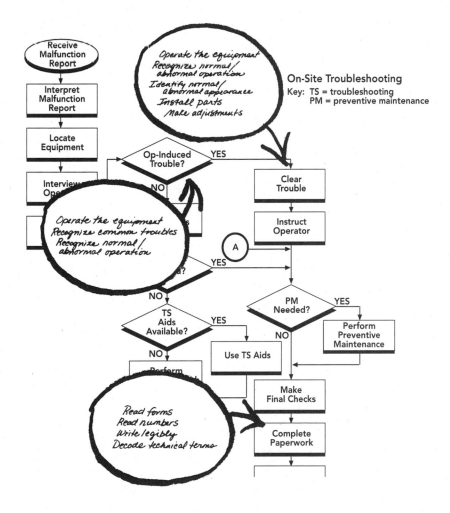

To Learn More: See Resources #1, #4, #12, and #15.

Part III

Deriving the Outcomes

7

Course Objectives

Situation: You want to draft descriptions of the important outcomes of the proposed instruction.

Your analysis has revealed that there are things your intended students (a) can't yet do that (b) they need to be able to do. Now it's time to describe the instructional outcomes (the need to do's); it's time to construct a verbal picture that will help guide you in developing the instruction and help guide your students in focusing their efforts. (This is not to suggest that you should avoid writing out your objectives until you have completed the analysis steps. Even if you do no analysis at all, it is still useful to reveal in writing what you want students to be able to do when they leave the instruction.)

What Are Objectives?

Objectives are a little like blueprints. They provide the guides that will guarantee that you are teaching what needs to be taught. And, because objectives describe *outcomes* rather than instructional process, they free developers and instructors alike to use all their ingenuity and creativity toward accomplishing those outcomes.

NOTE: Statements describing intended instructional outcomes are called objectives because their accomplishment can be measured. *Goals* are broad (fuzzy) statements of intent; *objectives* are measurable statements of intent. In plain language, if an outcome statement isn't precise enough to measure whether the outcome has been achieved, it isn't an objective.

Characteristics of Objectives

Here's an example of an objective to which you can refer as you read the characteristics described below:

Objective: Given an accident report form and an accident scene, be able to complete the report.

Criteria: a. All entered information is correct and legible.
b. Report is completed within 15 minutes.

1. An objective describes student performance. It doesn't say anything about what the instructor will do or try to accomplish. It doesn't describe course content or the textbook.

2. An objective is about ends rather than means. It describes a *product* of instruction rather than the *process* of instruction. It describes what students will be able to do when they are competent, rather than describing how they will be made competent.

3. An objective describes the key conditions under which the performance occurs on the job; i.e., the tools, equipment, environment, and circumstances that will influence the performance.

4. An objective describes the standard of acceptable performance; it tells how well someone must perform before being considered competent *on that objective.*

Each objective, then, will describe the (a) do what, (b) with what, and (c) how well:

    a. what someone should be able to do,

    b. the conditions under which the doing will occur, and

    c. the criteria by which the performance will be judged.

How Many Objectives?

You will need as many objectives as it takes to describe the important things you want students to be able to do. There will be one objective to describe each of the tasks you want students to be able to perform and one to describe each of the key skills they will need to learn before being ready to practice those tasks.

(There will be *no* objectives describing course content or the intended instructional process. To write objectives about anything but meaningful *outcomes* would swamp you in an unmanageable quagmire and would defeat the purpose of the objective. Objectives describe the ends. Items such as instructional content and practice material are means to the ends and go into the instruction rather than into the objectives.)

Each objective will be written in enough detail so that another professional instructor could turn out students who could do what you want them to do at the proficiency levels you prescribe.

Warning: Jargon Ahead

Over the past 25 years or so the notion of objectives has picked up jargon like a ship collects barnacles. They have been called behavioral objectives, competencies, outcomes, and performance objectives. Worse, the same objective has been labeled at one and the same time a classroom objective, a course objective, a school objective, a district objective, and a county objective.

But if you describe a measurable outcome important to accomplish, that is an objective.

Keep this in mind: they're not called behavioral objectives, because many describe the *product or result* of the behavior rather than the behavior itself. They're not called competencies, because competency means skill rather than intended outcome. The word *objective* doesn't need to be modified by the word *class, course, school,* or *county,* unless *different* outcomes are intended for those different entities.

If you describe an intended outcome specifically enough to tell whether it has been accomplished, call it an objective. Period.

How to Do It

1. Collect all the analysis documents drafted to this point.

2. While reviewing the task flowcharts, write an objective to describe the performance of each task.

3. Now look at the list of skills that anyone would have to have before practicing the entire task. Write an objective to describe each of those skills. In other words, write a statement to describe the limits of those skills, one that tells how much of each skill is needed by someone intending to perform the task. (Note: If you are an

experienced developer, write objectives only for those skills you are certain your students do not already possess.)

How much detail should you use? Just enough so that someone else reading the objective would understand it the way you do. How to find out? Show your draft to one or two people and ask them to tell you what they think it means. It doesn't matter if they don't understand the technical content of the objective. If they don't say what you want them to say, don't argue. Fix the objective.

4. Test your objectives for completeness. Each one will be good enough when you can answer yes to the following questions:

    a. Does it say what someone will be doing when demonstrating accomplishment of the objective (e.g., writing, solving, disassembling)?

    b. Does it describe the important conditions that will exist while the performing is being done (e.g., "given a wiring diagram"; "from memory"; "given an irate customer"; "using the tools available in the Happy Hair Styling Kit")?

    c. Does it tell how to recognize when the performance will be considered satisfactory (e.g., "it operates to within plus or minus two degrees"; "all customer objections have been addressed"; "correct to within one decimal"; "polished to a 63 finish")?

5. If you have completed one or more goal analyses during the task analysis, and if you listed one or more performances that students cannot now do, write an objective to describe each performance that will need to be taught.

6. If, as you draft your objectives, you find yourself writing one or more fuzzies, such as *understand, comprehend, appreciate, know, demonstrate,* or any other abstraction, complete a goal analysis for each fuzzy. Mark the performances that represent things students cannot yet do, and write an objective describing each of those performances.

Examples

Here are some examples of objectives. Note that though their form differs (some are written in a single sentence, others in two or more, and so on), they all say something about desired student performance, about the conditions under which the performance will be expected to occur on the job, and about how to tell when the objective has been accomplished (the criterion of acceptable performance).

Objective #1: Given any instructional objective, be able to identify (circle) the stated performance, the main intent, the conditions under which the performance will occur, and the criterion of acceptable performance, when these characteristics are present.

Objective #2: Given: A prescribed confined space, standard equipment, and two other team members.

Action: Carry out a confined-space entry and exit.

Criterion: Entry and exit will meet ATA-7 Safety Practices.

Objective #3: Given: A Model XXX System, standard tool kit, spares kit, and at least one symptom of a common malfunction.

Performance: Return the system to normal operation.
Criteria: The system functions within specs. There is no cosmetic or structural damage to system or to immediate area. No more than one unnecessary spare was used. No complaints were filed by client personnel.

Objective #4: Given a patient of any weight, be able to start an IV using no more than two needle punctures.

Goofing Off with Objectives

If it were not for the obfuscators, the preparation and use of objectives would be relatively simple. We would simply say what we want students to be able to do and then get on with developing instruction that teaches them to do it. Unfortunately, there is a gaggle of folks who like to make things harder than they are, who like to hang all sorts of danglies on the dashboard of their instruction. "Oh," you hear them saying as they look over your perfectly wonderful objectives, "now that you have written your classroom objectives, you must write course objectives, and then school objectives, and then the county objectives." Huh? They can't be serious! But yes, they actually do try to propagate the fiction that it is actually meaningful to say that a shovel is not only a shovel, but also a spade, a digger, a scooper, and a dirt-remover. I've seen dozens of honest instructors faced with this ridiculous task of rewriting the same objective to fit different jurisdictions. And I've seen them become frustrated, and then furious, as well they should.

There are other ways to goof off with objectives. One is to create a "taxonomy" of performance levels, so that instead of saying how well a person must perform, the objective simply says, "Level B3," or "Criterion level A2." This looks very precise, until you look at the definitions of these "levels." Then you discover that the criterion is still being kept a secret. Here's an example from one of these "criterion taxonomies." This one is called TPL-2 (Task Proficiency Level). This is how it is defined: "Can do most parts of the task. Needs help only on hardest parts. May not meet local demands for speed or accuracy." How well should a student be able to perform a task with this alleged criterion? You still don't know.

When you write an instructional objective, you are simply trying to communicate something about what you want students to be able to do when they leave you. That's all. If you want them to be able to unscrew a light bulb while rubbing their tummies, say so and be done with it. Don't let the bedazzlers drape your objectives with ornaments that are neither useful nor pretty.

Oh sure, you may find yourself having to conform to some bureaucratic demand to write your objectives in peculiar ways. If so, bend a little. Write a clean set that will be useful for your own instruction, and then rewrite them according to the "guidelines" you are expected to follow. Send those on up the line where they will do little harm.

To Learn More: See Resources #5, #11, and #12.

8
Skill Hierarchies

Situation: *You have drafted objectives that describe what you want students to be able to do at the end of your instruction. Now you want to know which objectives must be taught before others can be usefully attempted.*

Before plunging into development or improvement of the instruction itself, it will be useful to arrange your objectives into a picture that will show you how the objectives relate to one another.

Why Bother?

Suppose that you come to my class in brain surgery and, after offering an overview of the course, I anesthetize a couple of volunteers and ask you to show the class how to do a brain transplant.

"Wait a minute," you might scream in protest. "How can I do a brain transplant when I don't even know which instruments to use—or even how to get into the head—or how to get the brains out once I *do* get in? Hey, I'm not even sure where the brains *are* in these two numbskulls!"

Now, now, don't get excited. You've made your point. You noticed right off that the order in which things are taught can make a big difference in how well (and how quickly) students will reach mastery of the objectives. That's exactly why the hierarchy is so useful.

But there's more. Sometimes the order in which things are taught *doesn't* matter, and that can be even more valuable to know than where a specific learning sequence *must* be imposed. When the learning difficulty isn't impacted by the order in which the skills are taught, you can safely leave the sequencing decisions in the hands of your students (gasp!) so that they can attack the one that's best for them at the time.

Better yet, when some lessons require practice equipment, and, for example, you don't have enough atom-smashers to go around, your hierarchy will tell you how each student can be productively engaged while one is smashing a few atoms. So the skill hierarchy is a useful tool.

What's a Hierarchy?

A skill hierarchy is a picture that shows the prerequisite relationships between skills. It shows which are subordinate to others; that is, which must be learned before others can usefully be attempted. It also shows which are independent of one another; that is, which can be learned in any order. Just as the task flowchart visualizes the key steps and decisions involved in performance of a task, the hierarchy visualizes the *relationships* between the skills needed in performance of a task.

The task analysis *flowchart* says, "This step is followed by that step, which is followed by that decision, which is followed by that step." Thus, the flowchart describes a *process*.

In contrast, the *hierarchy* says, "This skill must be *learned* before that one can be learned," and "This objective is unrelated to that objective, and so these two objectives can be taught in any order." Thus, the hierarchy describes *relationships*.

Why Now?

Since you won't be sequencing your lessons (modules) into a course until after you've drafted them, why draft a skill hierarchy now?

Good question. Because you've just been thinking about, and drafting, the objectives of your instruction, you've got objectives on the brain. So it will be a little easier to simply go the next step and draft your hierarchy while you're hot.

There's another reason. Once you've drafted your hierarchy and TPop. (target population) description, you'll be able to decide on the prerequisites for your course. In other words, you'll be in a position to decide which skills you will teach in your course and which you will require students to bring with them when they arrive. This type of intellectual baggage is referred to as prerequisites and means, "I'm not going to teach it here; so if you want to benefit from my instruction, you'd better learn to do it before you come." Because you'll want to make the prerequisite decisions shortly after you draft your hierarchy, now is a good time to see what the hierarchy will look like.

What Does a Hierarchy Look Like?

A skill hierarchy looks very much like an organization chart (ugh!), except that instead of depicting the relationships between people, departments, and divisions, it depicts the relationships between skills. Here's an example.

Example #1: This hierarchy shows the skills that must be in place before someone can practice the entire task of baking a cake.

Figure 8.1

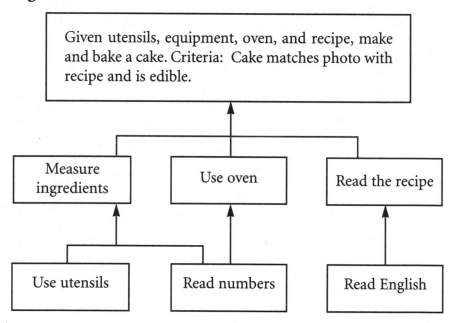

Read it from the top down, like this: Before being ready to practice the entire objective (baking a cake), anyone would have to be able to measure ingredients, use an oven, and read the recipe, and these three skills can be learned and practiced in any order. Before they can practice measuring ingredients, they need to be able to use utensils and read numbers, and these two skills can be learned and practiced in any order. And so on.

As we have all been victims of those who have *not* had the appropriate sub-skills in place before practicing the entire task, we should applaud the existence of the hierarchy and vigorously promote its use in the design of instruction.

Example #2: Before I show you another example, you may want to take a small Valium. I don't want to lose you to a bad case of hierarchy-shock. This next example is rather comprehensive and contains quite a few boxes and lines. So before looking at it get a blank piece of paper so that you can instantly cover all but a small piece of it. Got it? Okay, then, refer to the fold-out hierarchy at the back of this book.

This hierarchy shows the relationships between all the skills needed to troubleshoot a piece of electronic equipment. Don't let the apparent complexity of this hierarchy blow your socks off. Just look at it a piece at a time, just as you did the first one, reading from top to bottom.

> **NOTE:** The dotted lines shown at the right of the hierarchy identify skills that may or may not have to be learned, depending on the location of the job assignment.

Notice that the hierarchy does not say anything about any individual person. It shows what *anyone* would have to be able to do before being ready to practice the entire task. Once we know what *anyone* would have to be able to do, then we can match that picture with the existing skills of a particular individual and derive a curriculum for that person from the difference.

How Are Hierarchies Constructed?

It's really easier than it looks.

Suppose that on reviewing your task analyses, you find that students are going to have to learn to fill out certain forms in the performance of the job (whatever it may be). You note also that they are going to have to be able to read English.

Does one of these two skills—"fill out forms" and "read English"—have to be learned before the other can be learned? Or could you teach them in any order? Could students learn to fill out forms if they couldn't read them? Obviously not. So in this case the reading skill must be in place before the form-filling-out skill can be practiced. The little hierarchy would look like this:

Figure 8.2

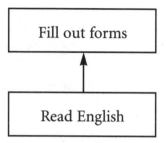

This tells us that all the skills shown leading into the box to which the arrow points should be mastered before that skill can be usefully attempted. We say that the reading skill *is subordinate to,* or *prerequisite to,* the "form-filling-out" skill. This does not mean that the reading skill is less important than the other. It means only that it must be in place before the other is attempted. It also tells us something else: It doesn't matter what an instructor alleges to be a preferred style of teaching, or a student professes to be a preferred style of learning; the hierarchy shows that one skill *must* be learned before the other—because one is part of the other.

Now let's consider another pair of skills. In reviewing your task analysis, you find that your sales students will have to be able to (a) describe product features to customers and (b) operate the product—let's say a car.

Would one of these two skills—"describe product features to customers" and "drive car"—*have to* be learned before the other could be attempted? That is, would I have to learn to describe the features of the car before I could learn to drive it? Or could I learn to drive without learning how to describe features to customers? I could, couldn't I? Both skills are important, but it wouldn't matter which was learned first. This hierarchy would look like this:

Figure 8.3

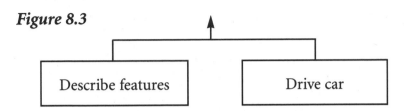

If you know which skills are independent of one another, you also know which sequencing options you could leave to the student if you so desired. In addition, you have information that will allow you to maximize course efficiency when you don't have enough practice equipment to go around. When practice equipment is limited, you can let your hierarchy tell you what students can *productively* work on while waiting their turn for the equipment.

How to Do It

1. Refer to the skills you derived from your task analyses. These are the skills you wrote to the right of the task steps that require them.

2. Delete the duplications from that list of skills. For example, it is likely that you will have written "Can read English" or "Can interview applicants" several times. If the *same* reading skill or interviewing skill is referred to in each instance, delete all but one of them. It makes no sense to "teach" a skill once it's learned.

3. Consider any pair of skills. Answer the question, Can these two skills be *learned* in any order? If so, draw them

side by side on your hierarchy. (A neat trick is to use those little pads of paper that are gummed on one end. Write each skill on one of the "stickies" and then move them around until you are satisfied.) If one must be learned before the other, the subordinate skill (the one that must be learned first) should be drawn below the other and connected to the one above it by an arrow.

4. Answer the same question for each pair of skills.

5. Draft a hierarchy; i.e., draw lines between the skills showing how they relate to one another.

6. Test your hierarchy.

    a. Make sure that every box on your hierarchy describes a skill rather than content. How? If you can put the word *can* in front of each item, it is probably describing a skill. For example, "Disassemble" makes sense when you add *can*—"Can disassemble." "Algebra," however, makes no sense at all when written, "Can algebra." Delete algebra and replace it with the skills that are relevant to the performance of the task in question. The subject matter won't get lost; it will go into your lessons. But subject matter has no place on the skill hierarchy.

    b. Starting at the top of the hierarchy, put a finger on each box that has one or more arrows leading into it and ask, "Is it true that students cannot practice this skill (the one you are pointing to) before they learn the skills shown as subordinate to this skill?" If the answer is "yes," go on to the next box and repeat the process. If the answer is "no," make the necessary correction.

c. Stand back and look at your hierarchy. If it is longer than it is wide, that is, if there are more levels from top to bottom than there are from side to side, it's likely that you have fallen into the trap of identifying process (steps in a task) rather than relationships (how skills relate to one another). Retest the hierarchy by repeating step 6b.

There is more to the matter of deriving hierarchies than can be described here. But the steps above provide the essence of the procedure.

To Learn More: See Resources #12, #15, and #16.

9

Target Population Description

Situation: You are ready to describe the key character-istics of the intended audience of your instruction, so that you can decide where the instruction should begin.

No doubt about it. "Target population description" is a piece of jargon right out of the late-night horror flicks. But not to worry. It means nothing more than "the students at whom your instruction is aimed." It could be called "audience description," but the word *audience* is generally reserved for a clump of people expecting to be entertained. Since we are not in the entertainment business (well, not officially, anyway), the word *audience* has misleading implications. As you run into the *target population description* verbiage below, just keep in mind that it refers to that particular gang of people for whom your instruction is intended, whether they are all alike or all different. So having swept the mystery aside, onward!

To this point in the string of analysis events, we have been considering procedures that will help us describe the end point, or outcomes, of instruction. With the information derived from the task, goal, and performance analyses, it will be possible to write objectives that describe what students should be able to do at the time they leave the instruction. (This is the topic of Chapter 7.) Now it will be useful to think about the "raw material" for the instruction, the students themselves. Just as the objectives will help determine where the instruction should end, the characteristics of the entering students will help determine where the instruction should begin.

Think of it this way: Instruction takes students from where they are to where they need to be, from their present state to a desired state. Thus, the instruction for any individual student should close the gap between actual and desired competence.

> What they need to be able to do
> – <u>What they can already do</u>
> = The instruction

You can see from this simple formula why the importance of a target population description cannot be overemphasized. Without it, the entry point for any student can only be arrived at by guessing.

What's in It for Me?

Target population information not only will help to reveal a useful starting point, it will help to shape the course itself. It will help determine which examples are most likely to fit, what vocabulary to use, and even what media and procedures to adopt. For example, if you learn that your students are active people, you won't make them sit passively for long periods of time. If you know they find reading difficult, you'll want to minimize the reading load by using other ways to present information. If they tend not to be interested in sports, you'll want to avoid examples from that area. If yours is a required course being attended by students who are "kicking and screaming" all the way, you'll want to make a special effort to ensure that students understand why they're there, and to motivate them to dig into the activities of the course.

BABY BLUES

© Reprinted with special permission of King Features Syndicate

If you spend even a tenth as much time thinking about and describing your students as you do thinking about your subject, you will develop a powerful tool for ensuring the effectiveness of your instruction. And you'll find some new ideas for increasing student interest in your subject.

"Wait a minute," you may be saying. "Does anybody actually do this target population thing?" You bet they do. Look in the folder of any accomplished instructional developer and you'll find several pages of prose describing the audience for the intended instruction. And the more diverse that audience, the more detailed the description. There's gold in them thar words (translation: detailed knowledge of the target population is one of the fastest roads to improved instructional efficiency and student motivation).

Like the other procedures described in this book, the target population description is yet another procedure that you can apply without requiring special permission or changes to policy.

How to Do It

1. Begin by reminding yourself that your TPop. description will be a working document that will not be published or seen by others. Remind yourself that it is not necessary to organize the content into categories unless that activity helps you to think.

2. Think about the students who will be entering your course, and write down everything you think you know about them. Write the items in whatever order comes to mind. Let one thing remind you of another. If you need help getting started, use these questions as triggers:

    What are their interests?

    Why are they taking this course?

    Do they want to be in this course?

What is their age range?

What will be the likely male-female split?

Do they have families?

What attitudes and biases do you expect them to bring?

What training and experience have they had in relation to the subject you teach?

Which of the skills listed on your task analysis do they already have?

What tools and equipment do they already know how to use?

What can you say about their physical characteristics?

What other responsibilities will continue during the course (i.e., are they expected to continue doing their job while learning)?

While they're in training, are they away from home, living in a hotel? How do they feel about their accommodations?

3. Describe the range of a characteristic wherever you can. For example, if you write, "Some will have graduate degrees, and some will be new to the subject," or "Some will have 20 years of experience while others will be new hires," you will know immediately that you will have to treat students differently if you are to be helpful to all of

them. To treat them all alike would be to bore some and frustrate others, and that's not your goal.

4. When you have said all you can say, keep the document handy. Add to it as items come to mind (while you're completing other steps in the development process). This is a working document that should grow as you go.

If you're thinking, "But I don't *know* anything about them because I never know who will enroll," you're kidding yourself. You may not know their exact characteristics, but you surely know a lot about the people who *won't* be coming to your course. Will you be teaching kings? Foreigners? Ph.D.s? Veterans? Opera singers? Come on. Sit down and say what you can about them. And if you *really* don't know anything about them, take a little time to find out. Talk to the registrar. Get some names and call them on the phone. Talk to them. They'll be delighted to tell you about themselves. And they'll be overwhelmed at the thought that an instructor actually cares.

When you can write two to eight pages that answer the questions on the checklist at the end of this chapter, you can conclude that you know enough about your students to design instruction for them.

NOTES:

• Describe them as they are, rather than as you wish they were. Write what they can actually do rather than an idealized version of those skills, e.g., "They're not all high school graduates," rather than, "They *should* be high school graduates."

• Describe people rather than institutions or policies. Say what people are like, rather than what the course will or should be like, e.g., "Most like to drink beer," rather than, "Company policy requires regular beer-drinking."

- If you think your students are all different, describe the ways in which they differ. Sure, they're all different. But most of those differences won't have anything to do with how you design instruction. Others will matter a lot. You spot the important differences by asking yourself whether the *same* instructional approach will fit for the entire *range* of the characteristic you are thinking about. For example, will the same approach work for baldies as well as for bush-heads? Sure. But will the same approach (treatment) work for readers as well as non-readers? For experienced as well as inexperienced? Less likely.

- Don't bother to organize what you write, and don't fret if you say the same thing more than once. Nobody's going to see this document.

Example #1: This example is organized under headings; the second one is more of a mind-dump. Both formats are equally useful.

TPop:	Sales Personnel
Course:	Computer Order Entry

Physical Characteristics

- These people range in age from 25-40.

- About half are male and half female.

- There are no apparent physical limitations.

- Most will be away from home, and the younger ones will be bleary-eyed from too much carousing the night before.

Formal and Informal Training

- All of the new hires will have at least a master's degree.

- The older reps will have more varied training. Some will have a degree, and others only a year or two of college.

- They will have 5-20 years of experience with the company.

- All are facile with English, and all are used to writing reports.

- All can read quite well.

- All are familiar with order-writing; they know company procedures and policies. They just don't know how to enter orders onto a computer terminal.

- The younger engineering grads will be familiar with computers; the older reps will not.

Anticipated Attitudes

- Many of the older reps are apprehensive that they will show up poorly against the younger people who use computers better than they do. They worry that they are old dogs who won't be able to learn the new tricks.

- The older reps will be somewhat resentful about being away from their territory for the duration of the course. They feel they could be making money instead of sitting in a classroom. Some feel that the computer will make order-writing take longer than it does now.

Interests

- Many students play golf with business colleagues— especially the older males.

- The majority are married, have families, and spend significant time socializing within the family network.

- They have a lot in common and tend to socialize within

the group as well. Though the older ones are apprehensive about learning to use computers, everyone hates the paperwork associated with writing orders.

- Most of the recent college graduates have had extensive computer experience and play with computers as a hobby. In particular, they spend time "surfing the net."

Sources of Reinforcement

- Many of the older "career" reps just do their jobs to collect a paycheck and receive little self-fulfillment from the job. They know they will never be promoted and no longer want to be.

- They are very protective of their territory—nobody's going to tell them what to do.

- The younger "flow-through" reps are enthusiastic about doing a good job and are pleased with themselves when they know they have done so. They will be promoted, and they know it.

- They are looking forward to the computer automation program. They are not wedded to the existing method and are eager to rid themselves of paperwork.

Example #2:

TPop:	Field Service Reps
Course:	Appliance Repair

- About 95 percent are male, and all are married.

- They range in age from 25 to 60.

- They are all strong enough to do the lifting and bending

required by the job. None have disabilities that would get in the way.

- They are not diet freaks, though some take regular steps to stay fit.

- All have completed high school, and a few have had a little college.

- Some have been in the military and received some electronics training there.

- Others have learned something of electricity or electronics through home-study courses or while working in dad's shop.

- Only a few have had appliance training before joining this company.

- Their interests include sports (football, bowling, basketball, fishing), TV, gambling, and ham radio.

- They don't jog or play tennis, golf, or chess.

- They are interested in computers, though many of the older ones are skeptical about their ability to learn much about programming.

- They are likely to have mechanically-oriented hobbies. These include ham radio, auto or motorcycle repair, and repairs around the house. They are all mechanically inclined and can handle hand tools with ease.

- They are not likely to read for pleasure, though they are not poor readers. They'd rather talk about "the trouble that got away" than read.

- They truly enjoy having control of their day. They like to decide how they will spend their time. They would much rather be on the road than in the classroom.

- They enjoy handling customer complaints, and they especially enjoy having a satisfied customer ask for them by name. They like to solve customer problems, but some aren't too skilled in customer interaction.

- Many like to tell themselves that they will soon start their own business, but few understand the implications of that challenge.

- They do not like to use test equipment or wiring diagrams in the presence of the customer, because they feel the customer will conclude they don't know what they are doing and that the repair will take a long time. They prefer to "wing it" rather than use test equipment.

- They prefer their training be "hands-on" rather than theoretical, and they badmouth any course that includes as much as 50 percent lecturing.

- About 20 percent will say they don't know why they've been sent to the course. These either think they are competent enough already or don't want to learn to handle a wider range of products. These are the reluctant dragons.

NOTE: The descriptions in these two examples contain several items that should influence the shape of instruction (content as well as procedures) designed for these students. If you find it hard to spot these cues, try this: Write a brief description of *your* own personal characteristics and then compare it to the characteristics of any course you've taken. The discrepancies between the way the course was run and the way it should have been conducted to maximize your learning reveal things the course developers should have taken into consideration before developing their course.

Goofing Off with Questionnaires

Questionnaires are *not* a useful source of information about your students. Why izzat, you may wonder? It's because it takes a great deal of skill and time to prepare a questionnaire that will elicit the type of information you may want. Items have to be drafted, and they absolutely must be tested and then revised, and maybe tested again, before one can have any assurance at all that the questionnaire tells you what you want to know. And people with this specialized skill are rare. If they are skilled in questionnaire development, they are not likely to be working in a training department.

If you just slap a questionnaire together, you aren't going to find out what you want to know, because it's hard to write items that aren't ambiguous. And when faced with ambiguous questions—or questions they think may be dangerous to their job—people will simply tell you what they think you want to hear. What you will do is create a great deal of paperwork for somebody—reproducing multiple copies, locating mailing addresses, affixing postage, and so on. You will also create work for someone who has to tabulate and/or analyze the "results." But those results will be mostly "garbage in—garbage out."

So unless you are looking for a way to expand your empire, consider the questionnaire as an impractical method for finding out about a target population. And don't use a questionnaire just because someone is bedazzled by data gleaned from large samples. It is far more productive, as well as faster and cheaper, to talk to a few people directly, either by phone, e-mail, or in person.

A Helpful Checklist

Check your target population description against the following list. Does it include information about:

1. age range?

2. sex distribution?

3. nature and range of educational background?

4. reason(s) for attending the course?

5. attitude(s) about course attendance?

6. biases, prejudices, beliefs?

7. typical hobbies and other spare-time activities?

8. interests in life other than hobbies?

9. need-gratifiers (i.e., what would reward them)?

10. physical characteristics?

11. reading ability?

12. terminology or topics to be avoided?

13. organizational membership?

14. specific prerequisite and entry-level skills already learned?

To Learn More: See Resources #2, #15, and #16.

10
Course Prerequisites

Situation: You have a clear picture of what students should be able to do when they leave you (objectives) and a picture (skill hierarchy) showing which skills must be learned before others can be attempted. You also have a good description of your target population. You can now derive the point at which it would be most appropriate to begin your course.

Here's another neat way to save development time while making sure that the finished course will do what you want it to. Just as you were systematic about deciding where the course should *end*, you want to be just as systematic about deciding where it should *begin*. Do it by using the procedure described in this chapter to answer the following questions:

Who will be qualified to enter my course? What, if anything, will they need to be able to do before they can benefit from my instruction? How can I select the least amount of content that will take students from their current skill level to mastery of the objectives?

Obviously, the *fewer* the restrictions on the entering student, the larger the number of people who will qualify for your course (and the more likely it will be that students will differ from each other in important ways). The *more* restrictions placed on the entering student, the *less* likely you will be to find people who meet your requirements (and the more likely they will be similar to each other). The trick is to write prerequisites that are realistic.

Let's Get One Thing Straight!

But let's get one thing straight. "Algebra 101" and "Abnormal Psych" are *not* prerequisites. They may be the names of a couple of courses, and they may be required for administrative reasons before someone may enter your course, but they don't qualify as prerequisites to your course. *A prerequisite is a skill that someone must have in order to benefit from your instruction.* If your course is taught in English, then students must be able to handle that language before they can benefit from your instruction. If you don't intend to teach in English, then an ability to understand the language is a prerequisite. If your course assumes that students already know how to solve algebraic equations that have one variable, then they will be less likely to benefit from your instruction if they enter it without that skill. If you don't intend to teach that skill, then it will have to become a prerequisite.

The *name* of a course tells nothing about the skills that students will have when completing the course. A course name describes only an administrative requirement that must be fulfilled; it says nothing about what students should be able to do before entering your course.

Where Do They Come From?

Prerequisites are derived during course development. Whenever you decide to *assume* that entering students will be able to do this or that, you are establishing a prerequisite. Why? Because prerequisites are formalized assumptions.

For example, when you say to yourself, "I'm not going to teach the math they should have learned last semester," it means you are going to *assume* that those math skills are already in place. If students who do *not* have those skills will be less likely to profit from your instruction, a rule should be established that says, "No one may enter this course without the following skills: . . . e.g., solve an equation; lift at least 50 pounds; climb a pole with climbing irons; name the bones of the body."

Be Realistic

You can see why it is important not to be arbitrary about the prerequisite skills you demand. On the one hand, if you make too few demands and allow everyone in, you will have to begin your instruction at square one. That may be impractical. On the other hand, if you require that too many prerequisite skills be brought to your course, you may not find anyone at all who qualifies. The goal is to be realistic.

Prerequisite skills should be demanded only when necessary. If you have no control over your incoming students and are expected to accept everyone who enters, it is silly to make demands about prior knowledge and skill. The realistic approach is to accept the students who appear on your doorstep and then begin your instruction where they are when they arrive. Sure, you'd rather teach the advanced stuff. But if the students don't have the basics, and if there is no one else to provide them, and if they need them before they can learn the advanced material, you have three choices:

1. Turn up your nose and say, "I'm not going to teach them what they should have learned elsewhere," and plow into the advanced material, wasting both your time and theirs.

2. Teach them the basics.

3. Find another way for them to learn the basics while you teach the advanced material.

So set up screening criteria (prerequisites), only when:

a. there are one or more things students should be able to do before entering your course, and

b. you have decided it's reasonable to expect them to be able to do them, and therefore you won't need to teach those things in your course.

How to Do It

1. Review the task analyses and the list of skills that anyone would have to have before practicing those tasks.

2. Review your target population description.

3. For each skill answer the question, "Is it reasonable to expect that entering students will already have this skill?"

4. If so, add that skill to your list of prerequisites, and design your course on the assumption that the skill will already be in place.

5. If it is not reasonable to assume that entering students will have this skill, decide how it will be taught—in your course or by some other remedial means?

6. Then, as you develop or modify your course, keep an *Assumption List* handy. Whenever you decide to assume that students will know something or be able to do something when they enter your course, add it to the list.

7. Write the prerequisites in the form of objectives.

8. Review your prerequisite objectives and make sure that each describes a skill rather than a course name (you are well aware of the wide variations in the way that any course can be taught by two or more instructors).

A Simpler Way

1. Review your skill hierarchy. (Remember that the hierarchy shows all the skills that *anyone* would have to have before practicing the skill shown at the top.)

2. Starting at the bottom, ask yourself whether it is reasonable to assume that your entering students will be able to perform the skill you are pointing to. For example, ask yourself whether it is reasonable to assume that they already can "Read English" or "Use hand tools" or "Add/subtract." (Refer to your target population description for guidance.)

3. If so, draw a circle around that skill.

4. If most or all of your incoming students can be assumed to have a given skill, consider that skill a prerequisite. That is, say to yourself, "I will assume that students can do this when they arrive and therefore I won't have to teach it in my course." Then decide what you will do about those few who do not have that skill—such as provide remedial material.

5. If you have been *told* what skills you must teach, but some of those skills don't *need* to be taught, tell yourself that you will only provide instruction in them for those who may need it.

6. Draw a line across the bottom of the hierarchy that expresses the rule: Skills above the line will be taught in

my course (or somebody else's course); skills below the line will be assumed to be brought by entering students and will therefore be considered prerequisites.

Example #1: After reviewing your TPop. description, you find that it is reasonable to assume that most or all incoming students will be able to use a computer word-processing application to write letters. So you base your instruction on that assumption. You decide not to teach students how to use the application. Instead, you will teach only the more advanced applications, and you will turn your assumption into a prerequisite objective, as follows:

Given a Spelgud word-processing application and one or more draft letters, enter and save the letters in the application.

Example #2: Refer to the fold-out hierarchy on the last page of this book. The target population for a course in troubleshooting consists of people who have had experience in working with a variety of equipment. Though their experience varies, it is reasonable to assume that all of them can perform the skills shown below the heavy line. Those skills, therefore, will not be taught. Instead, they will be considered prerequisites and entering students will be so informed.

To Learn More: See Resources #1, #5, #12, #15, and #16.

Part IV

Developing the Instruction

11
Criterion Tests

Situation: You have drafted objectives, a hierarchy, and a target population description. Now you want to develop the tools by which you can find out whether those objectives have been achieved—by which you can find out whether the instruction worked.

If it's worth teaching, it's worth finding out whether the instruction was successful. That sounds reasonable, doesn't it? After all, we weigh ourselves to find out whether we have achieved a weight target, and we test products to find out whether they are ready to ship to customers. In the same way, we measure the performance of our students to find out whether our instruction is doing what it's supposed to be doing.

The most direct measure of instructional success is to determine how many objectives were accomplished by each student. Enter the criterion test. The name is derived from the criteria stated in an objective. In practice, largely because the word "test" has such anxiety-producing connotations, criterion tests are usually referred to by labels more acceptable to the people using them. Skill checks and performance checks are common examples.

The purpose of the criterion test (skill check) is to determine whether an objective has been achieved, so that both student and instructor can determine what action to take next. If the criteria have been met, the student is encouraged to move to the next instructional unit. If the performance is weak, the problem is diagnosed and a remedy is suggested (usually more explanation or more practice). This use of a test is very different from the practice of "give 'em a grade and be done with 'em." The purpose is to help rather than to label.

When to Draft Skill Checks?

The time to draft skill checks is soon after you have drafted the objectives, but before you draft the instruction. There are two good reasons for this. First, drafting the skill checks soon after drafting the objectives will help you to clarify the objectives. Whenever you find yourself having difficulty drafting items that are correct for an objective, it will almost always be because the objective isn't yet clear enough to provide the necessary guidance. Clarify the objective, and the skill check items will fall into place.

Second, drafting skill checks soon after the objectives will also help you to focus your test items on the outcomes to be measured, rather than on the instructional process. It will help you to focus on writing items that will find out whether the outcomes have been achieved rather than on whether students can recognize or recite material that was covered during the instruction (except, of course, in those rare instances where recognizing and reciting are legitimate objectives).

"But three chapters ago you said I should draft my *hierarchy* after I drafted the objectives," I hear you screaming. "Which is it?" Easy there. Calm down. You can draft skill hierarchies or skill checks in any order; just make sure you do both things before you begin drafting relevant practice descriptions (which will be described in the next chapter).

Characteristics of Criterion Test Items

Test items that tell you whether an objective has been mastered have these two main characteristics: The test items match the objectives in both performance and conditions.

1. Each item matches the objective in *performance*. That is, the performance called for in the test item is the *same* as that called for by the objective; i.e., the item asks students to do what the objective says they should be able to do.

2. Each test item matches the objective in *conditions*. That is, it asks the student to perform under the same conditions spelled out in the objective.

The results of the test are evaluated by comparing the actual performance of the student with the criteria stated in the objective. This means that the student performance must achieve the same criteria as stated in the objective for that performance to be considered acceptable.

Why insist that a test item match the objective in performance? Let me answer that with another question. Why test at all? Your answer should be that you want to predict whether students will be able to do what you have taught them when they leave you. The best way to do that is to observe a sample of the *actual performance* you are trying to develop. Anything less than that won't tell you what you want to know. Think about it this way: Suppose your surgeon were hovering over you with gloved hands and the following conversation took place.

Surg: Just relax. I'll have that appendix out in no time.

You: Have you done this operation before?

Surg: No, but I passed all the tests.

You: Oh? What kind of tests?

Surg: Mostly multiple-choice. But there were
         some essay items, too.

You: Good-bye!

In practice it isn't *always* possible for your test items to duplicate the conditions called for by the objective. In such cases one approximates those conditions as closely as possible.

But it *is* always possible for a test item to demand the same performance as that described in the objective. For example, if an objective asks students to be able to repair equipment under water or to splice cables on top of a pole, it may not be possible to provide the water or the pole. In those instances you would provide the closest approximation to those conditions that you can. But you would *always* ask them to *repair,* and you would *always* ask them to *splice.* The rule is this: If you must, approximate the conditions, but *never approximate the performance.*

How to Do It

Prepare a criterion test for *each* objective whose accomplishment you want to measure. Many of those tests will consist of only one item (question), and the rest will need only three or four. How do you know how many items to include? The rule is this: The test will contain as many items as are needed to sample the range of conditions called for in the objective. Here are the steps for preparing a criterion test (skill check).

1. Read the objective and identify the performance (what it wants someone to be able to do).

2. Draft a criterion item that asks students to exhibit that performance.

3. Read the objective again and note the conditions under which the performing should occur (i.e., tools and equipment provided, people present, key environmental conditions).

4. Write those conditions into your test instructions.

5. For conditions you cannot provide, describe approximations that are as close to the objective as you can manage.

6. If you feel you must have more than one item to test an objective, it should be because (a) the range of possible conditions is so great that one performance won't tell you that the student can perform under the entire range of conditions, or (b) the performance could be achieved accidentally. But be sure that each item calls for the performance stated in the objective.

Example: For example, suppose I am teaching selling and my objective is that students will be able to follow the steps for closing a sale. And suppose I want that performance to occur in the presence of seven different kinds of customers (e.g., calm, angry, hostile, stupid, and so on). I would write an item to test performance involved in closing a sale that would be something like this:

a. Go to video room A, where you will find a product and a "customer."

b. Read the information sheet he or she hands you.

c. When you are ready, turn on the video recorder.

d. Using the product provided, try to close a sale.

Then I would talk to myself like this: "How many times would I want to see that performance before I would agree that students had accomplished the objective? Well, if they could do it once, I'd know they could *do* it, but if they did it only in the presence of a calm customer, I wouldn't know whether they could do it with a hostile one. I think if I had three samples of performance, I'd be satisfied they could handle the skill under the conditions specified."

Then I would write three criterion test items, *each of which calls for the same performance* under a different part of the condition range specified in the objective. In the example above, the items would all read the same, but the person playing the customer would be different. One would be hostile, one would be angry, and one would pretend to be a little dull. Most of the time, writing test items is simpler than the above paragraph implies. Here are some more examples.

Example #1: Suppose an objective reads:

Objective: Given a Model 12 keyboard, and a standard tool kit, be able to disassemble the keyboard down to the frame within ten minutes.

Let's follow the steps listed above.

1. What's the performance called for by the objective?

    Disassembling.

2. Draft a criterion test item.

    Disassemble this keyboard in ten minutes.

3. What are the conditions stated?

    The student is given a Model 12 keyboard and standard tool kit.

4. Add the conditions to the test item.

   On table 3 you will find a Model 12 keyboard and a standard tool kit. Use the tool kit to disassemble the keyboard down to the frame. You will have ten minutes.

5. Can all the conditions be provided as called for by the objective?

   Yes. No changes needed in the item.

6. Are additional items necessary?

   No. There is no range of conditions and little likelihood the performance could be correct by chance.

Example #2: Let's try another one. The objective says:

Objective: Given a malfunctioning Model 239 atomic bomb, one symptom, and a standard tool kit, be able to repair the malfunction within 30 minutes.

1. What's the performance called for by the objective?

   Repairing.

2. Draft a test item.

   Repair that atomic bomb.

(Example #2, continued on next page)

3. What conditions are stated?

    A malfunctioning bomb, one symptom, and a standard tool kit.

4. Add the conditions to the test item.

    You will find a Model 239 atomic bomb in room 10. The problem is that the detonator is showing an intermittent short. Use the standard tool kit provided to repair the malfunction. You will have 30 minutes.

5. Can all the conditions be provided as stated in the objective?

    Not on your life, they can't.

I can hear you shouting, "I am *not* going to give students *any* kind of bomb to be tested on no matter *what* the objective says!" Good for you. But while I can appreciate your feeling, you'd be only partly right. True, it would be impractical to provide the real thing here, even though trainees will be working on the real thing on the job. But that should never mean that you will ask for anything less than the performance called for by the objective, in this case, repairing. No matter what else you choose to do, you should ask the students to demonstrate repairing behavior, rather than talk-about-repairing or write-about-repairing. No multiple-choice exams, please. Only by having them perform per the objective can you find out whether the objective has been achieved.

It's the conditions you will modify, not the performance. So find the closest approximation to the real thing you can, and then ask for the actual performance on that. How about a wooden bomb of some sort? How about a real one that has had the oomph taken out of it? What's your best offer?

NOTE: If you write your test items according to the above procedure, and find yourself saying, "But the test items look pretty much like the objective," you need to have a little chat with yourself. Remember that the object of instruction is to bestow competence just as elegantly as you can manage to do it. The object of testing is to check to see if you've succeeded. The object of testing is not to use trick questions just to make it harder, or to spread people on a curve, or to find out whether students "really" understand. If your test items look similar to your objectives, rejoice. That's the whole idea.

The Multiple-Choice Trap

There is often a temptation to want to use multiple-choice and true-false items for testing competence. After all, didn't we spend an academic lifetime answering this type of item? Yes, we did. And aren't multiple-choice and true-false items easily scorable by scanners? Yes, they are. And isn't that a useful type of item for spreading students on a curve? Yes, indeed.

But all of that is irrelevant. The most reliable way to find out whether learners can change a tire is to ask them to do it. If you used multiple-choice or true-false items, you might find out what they *know* about tire-changing, but you won't find out whether they can do it. And if you wanted to use those types of items, who would write them? You? Who would do the item tryouts? You? Writing multiple-choice items is a specialty; it isn't easy to dash off a few items that are unambiguous and that test exactly what you want to test; without training in this skill you will be very likely to write items that don't follow good item-writing practice.

And who would do the scoring? You? If not, who will see to it that the test papers get to the scoring machine, and back again—in a timely manner? You see the trap. Just because someone refers to multiple-choice items as objective—which they are not—that doesn't make them useful, appropriate, or convenient. Worst of all, they practically never tell you whether your objectives have been actually achieved. Remember the surgeon who passed all the *written* tests on appendectomies?

Examples

Here are some examples of objectives, along with several possible test items for testing achievement of each. The test item that would be appropriate for testing achievement of the objective has been checked. The items not check-marked may tell you whether students can perform some part of the objective, but only the check-marked items will tell you whether they can perform as the objective demands.

Objective #1: Given your own computer terminal loaded with word-processing software, be able to type a business letter in accordance with the standards described in Company Manual 10A (page 23).

Test Items:

1. *Describe the five elements of a business letter.*

2. *On the attached letters, circle the typos and items not corresponding to company policy.*

3. *Tell how you would instruct a secretary in the preparation of business letters in accordance with company standards.*

✓ 4. *From the attached copy, type a business letter on your own terminal in the form described in Company Manual 10A (pg. 23).*

Objective #2:

Conditions: Given a Model 5 computer, standard tool and spares kits, a VOM, and at least one symptom of malfunction,

Action: Clear the malfunction.

Criteria: Computer is returned to normal operation and functions within specifications.

There is no cosmetic or structural damage to the computer or surrounding area.

All paperwork is correctly completed.

Test Items:

1. *Draw a block diagram of the Model 5 computer.*

2. *Explain how you would troubleshoot a Model 5 computer.*

3. *List the five most common troubles that happen to the Model 5 computer, and check those that are operator-induced.*

✓ 4. *The Model 5 computer in room 156 will not boot. Use the tools and spares that are in the room to clear the trouble. When you are finished, complete the Standard Trouble Call Report in the envelope labeled "STCR."*

Objective #3: Having written a goal you feel is worthy of achievement, be able to derive (write) the performances that, if exhibited, will cause you to agree that the goal is achieved (i.e., write an operational definition of a goal you feel is important to achieve).

Test Items:

1. *Describe the steps in completing a goal analysis.*

✓ 2. *Select a goal for your course and complete a goal analysis.*

3. *Review the completed goal analyses in the attached envelope. Circle the items that have been incorrectly described as performances.*

Objective #4: Given a disassembled M-16 rifle, be able to correctly assemble it, while blindfolded, within five minutes.

Test Items:

1. *List the parts of an M-16 rifle.*

2. *Describe the action of the M-16 rifle. Also state the history of the rifle and three combat situations for which it is the weapon of choice.*

✓ 3. *On the table in front of you is a disassembled M-16 rifle. Put on the blindfold and assemble the rifle. You will have five minutes to make the rifle completely operational.*

Objective #5: When approached by a prospective customer, be able to respond in a positive manner (i.e., by smiling, offering a suitable greeting, and by asking how you might be of service).

Test Items:

✓ 1. *Go to the videotaping room. When the instructor turns on the recorder, provide a suitable greeting to each of the "customers" who will enter the room.*

2. *Tell how you would respond in a suitable manner to a customer.*

3. *Write a description of a typical customer.*

Summary

To find out whether objectives have been accomplished,

1. Make sure your test items ask students to do what the objective asks them to be able to do, and

2. Ask them to do it under the conditions stated in the objective.

3. Then, when reviewing the performance, consider the objective achieved only when the performance matches, or exceeds, the criteria described in the objectives.

Finally, remind yourself that if you are going to the effort of using techniques intended to make instruction work, it is worth the effort to find out whether you've succeeded.

To Learn More: See Resources #10, #11, #15, and #18.

12
Relevant Practice

Situation: Before drafting instruction, you want to know what it will take to provide practice in the objectives.

As the trumpets tootle to the rumbling of the kettle drums, I enter to center stage and begin:

Me: Ladeeees and gentlemennnnn. Introducing the world's greatest magiciannn . . . YOU . . . ably assisted by the world's most handsome assistant . . . ME. (At which point you, wearing a flowing black cape and red tights, enter stage center . . . and proceed to look befuddled.)

You: *(Stage whisper to me)* Where's my magic apparatus?

Me: I left it in the garage.

You: You did what?

Me: I didn't think you'd need it.

You: *(Shouting in stage whisper)* And just how do you expect me to do my tricks without my magical apparatus?

Me: Hey! You're the magician!

All right, so maybe I lost my head to make a point, but the fact is that many things simply cannot be done without the "right stuff." And the right kind of practice is one of the most important "stuff" of all. After all, you can't practice making an elephant come out of a hat if you don't have a hat. Similarly, you can't practice the tuba if you don't have one, nor practice your golf if you don't have the balls for it.

Of course, most instructors know that practice makes perfect. They know that one learns to play the piano by practicing on the piano, rather than by talking about the piano or by answering multiple-choice questions about music. They know that the way to learn to interview or solve problems or to dance is to practice interviewing, problem-solving, or dancing. They know that practice is one of the powerful activities that makes their instruction work.

Less well understood is that the *nature* of that practice influences its usefulness.

Practice Makes Perfect, But . . .

Practice is a powerful way to develop skill, and a key component to making instruction work. But practice by itself is not enough! Practice without information (feedback) to the student about the quality of the practice can be worse than no practice at all. You already know why. Because students may spend a great deal of effort practicing and learning and getting better at the *wrong thing*. Therefore it is an instructional error (some call it fraud) (1) to withhold practice opportunities and (2) to allow students to practice without a suitable source of feedback.

Sources of Feedback

Feedback can be provided either by external or internal sources. Either you can build into the students' heads the ability to recognize correct from incorrect performance, or you can have another person or device do it. If you are going to build the performance criteria into the students' heads, then you must *prevent them from practicing until this is done.* Plainly put, unless you're going to provide an external source of feedback, they must not practice until they know how to evaluate their own performance.

If you will have an external source provide the feedback, you must be sure that the person or mechanism providing the feedback knows the performance standards. If another person is to provide feedback, that person must know more than just how to recognize correct and incorrect performance. That person must also be able to offer the information in a way that will not destroy the motivation or self-esteem of the student.

Practice Isn't Practice Unless ...

Suppose you saw me practicing the tuba and said, "Hi there. What are you doing?" And suppose I replied, "Why, I'm learning how to dance." What would you think? Suppose I then said, "Y'know, I've been working hard at this, but my dancing doesn't seem to be improving. Got any ideas?" I think your reply would be obvious: "If you want to learn how to dance, you need to practice dancing." And of course you'd be right—and I'd thank you for not using saltier language in your reply.

That is an obvious example of wrong (useless) practice. Other examples are a little harder to decode. Suppose while learning to be a policeman you are expected to learn when and when not to shoot (a rather important skill). And suppose the instructor had you practice reciting the law that pertains to shooting. Would that practice help you get better at making the shoot/no-shoot decision? You see that it isn't as easy to decide in this case. Actually, knowing the law may be useful information, but it won't improve your ability to make the instant decisions that shooting situations require. It wouldn't, in other words, provide *relevant* practice of the skill in question.

Before deriving the content of your instruction, therefore, you should describe the "right stuff" that will be needed for practice of each objective. Not only will that make it easier to derive the instructional content of the lessons (modules), it will make the actual development process go faster.

How to Do It

Here's how to describe relevant practice for an objective. Once you've done it for six or so objectives, it will only take a minute or two to do it from then on.

1. *Performance.* Write down what the student would be doing when practicing the essence of the objective.

   Example: If the objective says, "Be able to assemble schlorks . . .," you would write "Assemble schlorks."

   Example: If the objective says, "Be able to write a computer program," you would write "Write computer program."

2. *The right stuff.* Write down the things (the right stuff) that you would have to provide in order to make the practice happen. (The objective will tell you.)

   Example: If the objective says, "Given a set of parts and a standard tool kit . . . ," you would list "Set of parts" and "Tool kit."

   Example: If the objective says, "Given a prospective customer and a product to sell . . .," you would write "Prospective customer," and "(insert the name of the product)."

3. *Adequacy feedback.* Write down how you will provide feedback (information) about the adequacy of the practice performance (whether it's OK or not OK).

   Example: If the performance can be compared against a list of right answers, write "Answer key."

   If the performance can be evaluated against a checklist that describes the key characteristics of the performance, write "Checklist of criteria or key points."

   Decide whether, given the right answers, or checklists, or modeling, or descriptions of desired performance, students could decide for themselves whether their performance is OK or not OK (adequacy feedback). If they could, let them. If they couldn't, you will have to decide how to provide an external source of feedback (e.g., another person).

4. *Diagnostic feedback.* Now you need to think about who or what will diagnose performance that is not yet OK. That means thinking about who or what will determine what's wrong with the performance, and how the diagnostic feedback will be provided to the student. Answer this question:

   If the student knows that the performance isn't yet good enough, could the student decide what is wrong with it?

   If so, you're done with this step. If students can't be counted on to decide what's wrong with their performance, you will have to provide an external source of diagnostic feedback (e.g., another person).

5. *Corrective feedback.* If students know what's wrong with their practice performance, will they know what to do to fix it? If so, that's all you need to do. If not, you'll need to provide an external source of information about how to correct the performance (e.g., another person; written description of common problems; checklist of probable remedies).

6. The final step is simply to take your answers to Items 1-5 and draft them into a short description of relevant practice for each objective. This description may be as short as one that says, "Provide tools, schematics, faulty thermostat, list of tolerances of adequate operation. Student will practice repairing. Instructor will provide diagnostic and corrective feedback." Sometimes more "right stuff" will have to be provided to make the practice relevant to the objective, possibly including an instructor or other student to supply feedback by observing the practice while making marks on a checklist.

Whatever the result, the importance of practice—*relevant* practice—cannot be over-emphasized. As you well know, *doing is the key to competence.* Since the conditions under which the doing takes place can be critical to student improvement, it pays to complete this step in the development process with care, no matter what or where you are teaching. It usually takes only a few seconds after some practice.

NOTE: Sometimes you will need little or nothing to provide the conditions for relevant practice. When this happens, you may tend to feel as though you've done something "wrong" or forgotten something. When that happens, try this: Imagine your student in an empty room and then ask yourself what you will need to provide to make it possible for that student to practice the objective. If it's only a pencil and a piece of paper, so be it. If it's only a musical score, so be it.

RELEVANT PRACTICE CHECKLIST

PERFORMANCE

1. What will trainees be doing when practicing the objective?

> *Replacing parts*

2. What do the criteria in the objective talk about?

- Product of performance → | Save the Product | ✓
- Shape of performance → | Record the Performance | ✓

CONDITIONS

3. What cues/conditions must you provide to make the practice possible (i.e. to meet the conditions stated in the objective)?

> *R-bander engine   manual*
> *bench   parts*
> *tools*

FEEDBACK

4. How will you let trainees know their performance is OK or not OK (i.e. meets the standards of the objective)?

(Check as many times as needed.) →

• Description of correct responses	
• Modeling of desired performance	
• Checklist of criteria or key points	✓
• Description of desired performance	
•	

ADEQUACY

5. Given those standards, can you rely on trainees to decide if their performance is OK or not OK?

(YES) — NO → | Have somebody (or something) provide the comparison of performance with standards | ☐

DIAGNOSTIC

6. If the work is NOT OK, can you rely on them to decide what is wrong with the performance?

(YES) — NO → Could they tell what's wrong if you model the performance and/or describe common problems?

If YES . . . | Provide modeling and/or description of common errors (problems) | ☐

If NO . . . | Have somebody diagnose the performance | ◯

7. If they know what is wrong with their performance, can you rely on them to know what to do to improve?

(YES) — NO → Would they know how to improve if you modeled the performance and/or described typical remedies or solutions?

If YES . . . | Provide modeling and/or description of typical remedies or solutions | ☐

If NO . . . | Have somebody provide the remedies or solutions | ◯

CORRECTIVE

8. Describe relevant practice. Account for all the checks made above, and include all items needed to provide the cues/conditions listed in item 3.

© The Center for Effective Performance. From *Instructional Module Development,* by R. F. Mager. 2nd Edition, Revised 1996.

Here are some examples:

Example #1:

> *Objective:* Be able to replace any component in an R-Bander aircraft engine. Conditions: shop environment, tools and manual available. Criterion: No damage to tools or engine; replacements are made according to R-B procedures.

Thinking it through: (The checklist on the following page is a job aid often used in the preparation of relevant practice descriptions.) The numbered items below refer to the numbered items on the checklist.

1. "Let's see. The performance called for is that of replacing parts.

2. "The criteria talk about the performance itself (replacements are made according to R-B procedures) *as well as the product of the performance* (correctly replaced parts as well as undamaged tools and engine). That means I should record (e.g., videotape) the performance so that it can be reviewed later.

3. "To make practice possible, I'll have to provide an engine on a bench, some tools, some replacement parts, and the manual. Oh, yes; I'll also need a video recording setup. That way students can evaluate their own practice performance.

4,5. "Now about adequacy feedback. How can I provide the basis for letting students decide whether their performance is OK or not OK? Hmm, I can provide a checklist of key items. That way they can review their videotape to see whether their work matches the checklist items.

6. "Now about diagnostic feedback. If their work is not OK, will they be able to recognize what's wrong with it? Yes, I'm sure they will.

7. "And finally, corrective feedback. If they know what's wrong with their performance, can I count on them to know what to do about it? Yes, in this instance I can."

And that's it. My relevant practice description will look like this:

Relevant Practice Description:

Provide: R-Bander engine
Bench conditions
Tools
Manuals
Replacement parts
Checklist of key points
Video recording setup

Procedure: While being video-recorded, students will be asked to replace a series of parts. For feedback, they will review the tape and match their performance to a checklist of key points.

NOTE: The procedure is the same for any objective, regardless of whether it requires practice with hardware, various forms of human interaction, problem-solving, creativity, etc. Because relevant practice is the key to the development of competent performance that will endure in the face of adversity and the ravages of time, it is important to use a systematic procedure in the description of relevant practice. That way you won't leave out any of the key ingredients.

RELEVANT PRACTICE CHECKLIST

PERFORMANCE

1. What will trainees be doing when practicing the objective?

Writing relevant practice descriptions

2. What do the criteria in the objective talk about?

- Product of performance → Save the Product ✓
- Shape of performance → Record the Performance

CONDITIONS

3. What cues/conditions must you provide to make the practice possible (i.e. to meet the conditions stated in the objective)?

Objective
Checklist
Something to write the description on

FEEDBACK

4. How will you let trainees know their performance is OK or not OK (i.e. meets the standards of the objective)?

(Check as many times as needed.) →

• Description of correct responses	
• Modeling of desired performance	✓
• Checklist of criteria or key points	✓
• Description of desired performance	
•	

ADEQUACY

5. Given those standards, can you rely on trainees to decide if their performance is OK or not OK?

(YES)

NO → Have somebody (or something) provide the comparison of performance with standards

DIAGNOSTIC

6. If the work is NOT OK, can you rely on them to decide what is wrong with the performance?

YES

(NO) → Could they tell what's wrong if you model the performance and/or describe common problems?

If YES . . . Provide modeling and/or description of common errors (problems) ✓

If NO . . . Have somebody diagnose the performance ○

CORRECTIVE

7. If they know what is wrong with their performance, can you rely on them to know what to do to improve?

(YES)

NO → Would they know how to improve if you modeled the performance and/or described typical remedies or solutions?

If YES . . . Provide modeling and/or description of typical remedies or solutions

If NO . . . Have somebody provide the remedies or solutions ○

8. Describe relevant practice. Account for all the checks made above, and include all items needed to provide the cues/conditions listed in item 3.

Here is one more example.

Example #2: For an example of a totally different sort, let's use the skill of writing relevant practice descriptions.

Objective: Given an objective and a checklist, be able to write a description of relevant practice. Criteria: The description includes (a) the performance required, (b) critical cues and conditions under which the performance is expected to occur, and (c) sources of adequacy, diagnostic, and corrective feedback.

Thinking it through:

1. "Let's see now. The performance called for is that of *writing* a relevant practice description (#1 on the checklist on the preceding page).

2. "All the criteria describe the product of the performance, so there would be no need to record the performance for later review; that is, the objective calls for a written description rather than for the behavior that leads to that description. I'll save the product (the written description).

3. "To make practice possible, I'll have to provide one or more objectives for students to practice on and some checklists. That's about all.

4. "How can I provide the basis by which they can decide if their descriptions are OK or not OK? I can provide a model of a description. It would also help them decide whether their description is OK or not OK if I provided a completed checklist.

5. "Could students compare their descriptions with those two items and decide whether their performance is OK or not? Yes, they could.

6. "There's no problem about diagnostic feedback. If their performance is not OK, they can decide what's wrong with it, provided that I provide them with a model of a well-written relevant practice description and a description of the common errors.

7. "Would they know how to correct their work, given the model, the checklist, and the description of common errors? Yes, I know for certain they could do that. Therefore I don't have to provide an instructor or someone else to do it for them. And that's it. I'm now ready to write a brief description of what it would take to provide relevant practice."

Relevant Practice Description: To make practice possible, I need to provide (a) objectives, (b) checklists, and (c) something to write the description with and on. For feedback, I need to provide a model of the correct descriptions, completed checklists for each objective, and a description of common errors.

> **NOTE:** Though it takes only minutes to prepare brief relevant practice descriptions for a batch of objectives, it is a key step in the development process. Without it, it's just too easy to provide wrong practice, partial practice, or no practice at all in the important skills that need to be learned.

To Learn More: See Resources #13 and #16.

13
Content Derivation

Situation: You have derived objectives and know what it will take to provide relevant practice in those objectives. Now you want to derive the content that will bridge the gap between what students can already do and what they will need to know or do before being ready to practice the objective.

Content derivation is about closing gaps; it's about closing gaps between what people can already do and need to be able to do. Obviously (I hope), if there is no gap—no difference—between what they can do and need to be able to do, then there's no need for instruction. There's no need to impose on their, or your, valuable time to "teach" them what they already know.

That's a pretty powerful idea, because if it were actually put into practice, the amount of instruction in the world could be reduced at least by half. (Remember all that time you spent in classrooms expected to "learn" what you already knew?) So why don't we put it into practice? Two main reasons.

Why We Don't

Mostly for administrative convenience, we've traditionally clumped our instruction into "lessons" spanning a pre-determined amount of time, usually fifty minutes. This fifty-minute burst of instruction is usually referred to as a "period." Because of this fixed-time lesson period, we've been snookered into filling it with instruction, whether it was needed or not. You remember how it went:

"I need to teach my students how to fill out these forms."

"How long will that take?"

"Not more than ten minutes, so I'll have to think of something else with which to fill the rest of the period."

"Why don't you just dismiss them and let them get on with their lives?"

"Hey, I can't just let them go after they've learned what they need to know."

"Why not?"

"Well, if somebody caught them wandering in the halls, or found out I was letting them go 'early,' I'd probably be fired." (Note: Some people refer to this situation as Adult Day Care.)

"Oh."

There is another reason for excess instruction. Traditionally, courses have been content-driven. That is, they have been designed to teach as much content as the allotted time would allow. As there is never any shortage of content, there is always enough to fill the periods. ("Hmm. I'll include the first three chapters . . . leave out the fourth one . . . but be sure to include Chapter 7. That's my favorite topic . . . and besides, that topic has always been included in this course . . .")

Instruction Fills a Gap

Now instruction is designed to fill a need; rather than being designed to fill time, instruction is designed to accomplish important outcomes. This change in approach has changed the definition of a lesson:

Then: A lesson consisted of whatever amount of instruction filled a fixed time period. Thus, one student may need ten minutes to accomplish one objective, and another may require two hours, but what they got was a fixed time period. During a traditional lesson period, then, a student might master one or two objectives or only part of an objective. Time was fixed, and performance levels achieved were variable.

Now: A lesson consists of all the instruction and practice required to accomplish an objective. Thus, a lesson consumes whatever time it takes to reach mastery of an objective. To avoid confusion, this kind of lesson is called a "module" and includes all the stuff (instruction, demonstrations, practice) needed to promote mastery.

Selecting Content

Knowing that there is more to know than time to teach it— or interest in learning it—we are led to the conclusion that some content must be selected in, and some selected out; that choices will have to be made. How shall these choices be made? Actually, it's relatively easy.

You know what the important outcomes of the instruction should be, and you know more or less what your students will be able to do when they arrive. You know what "stuff" is available to you in the place where learning will occur, and the restrictions under which you will have to work. And you know what you will need to do to make relevant practice possible.

Deriving content for your instruction, therefore, amounts to reviewing the requirements for relevant practice, your target population description, and your hierarchy, and answering the question:

"Why aren't they ready to practice this objective NOW?"

What prevents them from being ready to practice as soon as they "enter" the module? The answer to that question will tell you what needs to be done to fill the gap between what students can now do and what they need to be able to do before being ready to practice the entire objective of the module.

The secret to deciding what to put in and leave out is to think about module content as the difference between what is already known and what needs to be known.

> What needs to be known
> – <u>What is already known</u>
> = What needs to be taught

Why Aren't They Ready to Practice Now?

Usually, when students aren't prepared to practice as soon as they enter a module, it is because there is something they don't know, such as *how* to do what they're expected to do, or because there are some safety precautions to learn or common errors they should be able to avoid, or because they don't yet know how to recognize what the desired performance looks and feels like (you don't want them to practice until they can monitor their own performance).

Sometimes, they aren't ready to practice now because they don't believe that what they're supposed to learn is valid; they don't believe it will work. For example, those who don't believe that self-managed work teams work aren't ready to practice working in such an environment. Something needs to be done before initiating practice exercises to convince them that such work teams do indeed work. (Perhaps a demonstration or a game would be appropriate.)

The Hard Part

The *procedure* for deriving content is relatively simple. The hard part is getting used to the idea that the current lesson probably contains quite a bit more content and activities than needed to accomplish the objective. (Not long ago my colleagues and I found that a group of manager trainees would become better performers if a well-tabbed three-ring binder of information were used to replace the *entire* 18-week course they were required to attend. This is not to suggest that any or all of *your* courses should or could be replaced by a job aid; it is only to remind you that efficient instruction often requires that at least some content in an existing course be dropped. Or saved for another course.)

You know how it goes. We all have our favorite topics, war stories, anecdotes, and demonstrations. We like the subject we are teaching, and we are all wrapped up in it. That being the case, discovering that some or all of what we do in the classroom can be better done *without* can be something of a blow to the ego. But if we are serious about making our instruction work, and work as efficiently as we can make it, then we need to think of those "extras" as obstacles rather than as necessities.

Module Components

Before being ready to practice content derivation, you need to have a list of module components. This list can be used as a job aid to remind you of the components that you should almost always include in a module and those that you might include. In the list of module components that follows, the items you should almost always include are shown in bold italics:

Prepare to Practice

These are components used to get students to the point where they are ready to practice the objective:

- ***Objective***

- ***Skill check description***

- ***Description of relevance (to the student)***

- Modeling (demonstration) of competent performance

- Instructional content (e.g., explanations, demos)

- Alternate resources

Relevant Practice

- ***Practice***

- ***Feedback***

Directions

- *Labels (e.g., module name and/or number)*

- *Directions to students (e.g., Go get . . .).*

- Directions to other instructors (e.g., To teach this unit you'll need the following materials, etc . . .).

Evaluation

- Self-checks

- *Skill check*

- *Self-evaluation explanations*

As you can see, the basic "floor plan" of a module is one that, at the front end, always informs students of the purpose and relevance of the lesson, and at the back end, always provides practice, feedback, and evaluation. In between, it offers whatever instruction is needed to get them from where they are to where they are ready to practice.

How to Do It

Now we're ready to consider the content-derivation procedure.

1. Review the objective.

2. Review your description of relevant practice for that objective.

3. Review your target population description and hierarchy, and note what students can already do when they enter this module.

4. Now answer the question, "Why aren't they ready to practice this objective *now*, at the time they begin work on the module?"

Imagine that a student has read the objective of the module and understands the importance of learning what the module has to teach. Why would that student not then be ready to practice that objective right then and there? That's the question to answer. To make it easier, break the question into smaller ones:

a. Do you believe they aren't ready to practice because they don't yet know *how* to do what they need to do? If so, what do they need to know how to do?

b. Do you believe they aren't ready to practice because there are one or more common errors they are likely to make in their present state of readiness? *Which* common errors?

c. Are they not yet ready to practice because they haven't yet been taught how to avoid certain dangerous situations? *Which* situations?

d. Are they not ready to practice because they don't yet know how to tell when their practice performance is OK or not?

The answers to these questions will tell you what content to include. Of course, if there is some "standard" content that isn't needed for answering these questions, **leave it out.** If you happen to leave something out that should be in, you'll find that out when you test the module. (Note: The reverse is not true. If you put something in that should be left out, testing may not expose it. So it's always better to start "lean" and add content and activities where necessary.) So there's little need to worry about making your instruction too skimpy.

NOTE: Here's an important tip on how to complete this step in the development process. Think of yourself as constructing a *summary* of lesson content, rather than an outline of content. Sure, your content will be presented in an organized manner when the module is *finished,* but it can be an obstacle to begin outlining before you have any substance to outline. So just list the content of the module as you answer the questions above. And when you find that for some objectives you will need only to provide practice and feedback, reward yourself. Your students will thank you for refraining from boring them with things they already know, and, if they're an enlightened lot, your administrators will thank you for getting the job done with a minimum of wasted motion.

"But I couldn't let my students out early," I hear you gasping. Of course not. After all, we're not *that* enlightened. But you *can* provide a menu of optional activities that students would find interesting and productive if they reach competence before the time is up. Or, you could teach them how to do a performance or goal analysis. *Everybody* ought to know how to do *that.*

Warning: Danger Ahead

The technique described in this chapter is a powerful one. Use it for the course that you develop, but be cautious about applying it to someone else's. Though you will be able to identify all sorts of unnecessary instruction once you've learned this technique, you would be wise to share that knowledge with great care. Nobody likes to be told that there is no need for some—or all—of what they are teaching.

Examples

Below are two examples of the content derivation procedure. The first contains a subject with which you're not likely to be too familiar, so you won't already be expert at the skills involved.

Figure 13.1

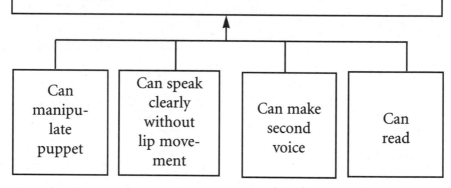

Given a script and a puppet, be able to act out the script. Criteria: The voices originate from the correct source, both vent and puppet react appropriately to the other's lines, and the vent does not anticipate (i.e., turn toward the puppet before the puppet begins to say a line).

| Can manipu- late puppet | Can speak clearly without lip move- ment | Can make second voice | Can read |

Example #1: Ventriloquism involves a blending of the skills of manipulation (operating the puppet), voice, and lip control. Assuming students can read a script, once these three sub-skills are mastered they're ready to learn how to act out a script. Here's the objective, along with the hierarchy to show which skills must be in place before they enter this module. (By the way, ventriloquists often refer to themselves as "vents.")

Relevant Practice Description: Students will be provided with:

- a script,

- a puppet, and

- video equipment.

For feedback, they will review (with a coach) a videotape of their performance.

Content derivation: Having completed modules involving practice in the sub-skills, students now enter the module that will teach them to act out scripts. Why aren't they ready to practice as soon as they enter the module? They already know how to read, how to produce a voice for the puppet, how to speak using lip control, and how to manipulate the puppet's controls. So why aren't they ready to practice acting out a script?

They're not quite ready to practice because they may not know how to recognize correct performance when they see and hear it; that is, they may not yet be able to recognize a properly acted script. Any other reason they aren't ready to practice? None whatever. This is what a module to teach this objective would contain:

List of Module Content:

- The objective
  This is what you should be able to do . . .

- Performance-check description
  Here's how we'll check your competence . . .

- Description of relevance (rationale)
  This is why this skill is important to you . . .

- Demonstration of correct performance
  Here's what it looks and sounds like when done correctly . . .

- Practice in recognizing correct performance
  This will help keep you from practicing the wrong thing . . .

- Practice in performing, with feedback
  Now it's your turn . . .

- Skill check
  Let's find out how well you're doing . . .

(Ironically, ventriloquism provides a good example of how the *absence* of a critical piece of information can slow development of the skill. The critical information missing from every course I've seen is this: *The ventriloquist can never hear the illusion!* No matter how much they may practice, they will never "hear" the puppet's voice coming from the puppet, because they themselves are making that voice. Once this fact is known by the students they don't feel nearly as silly "talking to themselves;" they're more likely to practice, and they develop confidence in their skills much faster.)

Example #2: Let's use one of the same examples we used for relevant practice. Here's the objective again and the description of relevant practice for that objective:

Objective: Given an objective and a relevant practice checklist, be able to write a description of relevant practice. Criteria: The description includes (a) the performance required, (b) critical cues and conditions under which the performance is expected to occur, and (c) sources of adequacy, diagnostic, and corrective feedback.

Relevant Practice Description: Students will be provided with:

- practice objectives,

- checklists, and

- paper to write on.

They'll be asked to write a relevant practice description.

For feedback, they'll be provided with:

- a model of a correct description,

- completed checklists for each practice objective, and

- a description of common errors.

Content derivation: Assume that the target population consists of people who have learned the skills described in the earlier chapters of this book. Now they are entering a module that intends to teach them how to derive descriptions of relevant practice from any objective. What should that module include? Without batting an eye, you should answer, "Practice." Right. No matter what else it includes, it will include practice in the objective and feedback (information) about the quality of the practice performances.

What else? Why can't these people practice the minute they walk into the module? Let's see . . . they already know how to use the relevant practice checklist. But they may not understand the importance of the procedure. Second, they may not know when to do it.

Anything else? No-o-o-o . . . wait. Common errors. Without some help they are likely to decide that they will need an instructor to provide feedback, when a less-expensive medium would do as well or better. Some practice examples using the checklist will prepare them to describe relevant practice effectively. And that's about all.

So here is what the module should include:

List of Module Content:

- The objective
  This is what you need to be able to do . . .

- Skill check description
  Here's how we'll check your competence . . .

- Description of relevance (rationale)
  This is why this skill is important to you . . .

- Explanation of the procedure and examples of the final product of the performance (i.e., some relevant practice descriptions)
  Here's how it's done . . .

- Practice with a series of objectives
  Now it's your turn . . .

- Skill check
  Let's find out how well you're doing . . .

The easiest way to learn the skill of content derivation is to practice by applying the procedure to someone else's objectives (quietly and discreetly). That way you'll get to practice the skill without having your ego bruised at the same time.

To Learn More: See Resources #5, #15, and #16.

14
Delivery System Selection

Situation: Having summarized the content for the modules, you are ready to decide how the instruction will be made available (delivered) to the students.

Now we arrive at what is probably the easiest part of instructional development, that of deciding what combination of things we will use to present the instruction and practice to the student. Though there is a priesthood that advocates charts and diagrams and that would have you believe this is a complicated affair, it isn't, for two main reasons. The first one is that you won't have so many choices available to you that you need a chart to help you decide which to use. Bluntly, if you only have two pairs of socks, it isn't hard to decide which to wear. The second reason is that by the time you have listed the things (materials, media, equipment) you need in order to provide practice and feedback, you'll seldom need anything more.

Why Delivery Systems?

So let's think a little about delivery system selection. First off, instructional technologists talk about delivery system selection rather than about media selection. That may seem as though they're using big words when smaller ones will do, but there is a reason. Media are message carriers: overhead projectors, chalkboards, computers, books, telephones, etc. They are the things on which you "write" the information you want to get to your students.

That's fine, except that we use more than those media to present instruction to our students. We often use people, either to present information, to participate in practice requiring one or more other people, or to assist in providing feedback. In addition, we often use "job things," such as machinery or equipment, to assist with instruction and practice. We use real automobiles for practicing auto mechanics and driving, real heads when practicing barbering, and real rifles when practicing marksmanship. Though these are critical requirements for proper presentation of the instruction, they are not media in the usual sense of that word. Hence the preference for "delivery system selection" rather than "media selection."

Features vs. Benefits

You already know most of what you need to know to select a suitable delivery system for the pieces of your course. You know the features of most of the available media, and you know what they are used for. That's a big leg up. Before we move on, though, it would be useful to think a moment about delivery system benefits.

One feature of hydrochloric acid is that it will eat through metal and cloth. Is that a benefit? Depends on what you're trying to accomplish. If you're trying to etch metal, it might be an advantage. If you're trying quench your thirst, it is definitely a disadvantage.

One feature of a lathe is that it can make round things. Is that an advantage? Depends on what you're trying to accomplish. If you're trying to make a table leg, it's an advantage. If you're trying to make a tin box, it's a useless feature.

One feature of a videotape is that it can call up a picture or motion sequence instantly. Is that an advantage? Depends on what you're trying to accomplish. If you're trying to present an illustration or demonstration, it can be an advantage. If you're trying to give students practice in tying knots, it is of little value.

So a feature of a delivery system is a characteristic. A feature becomes a benefit *only* when it will help accomplish a purpose. (If you keep that in mind, it will help you cut though the razzle-dazzle pitches of the bedoozlers and help keep your instructional costs down.)

Delivery System Selection Rule

Having said that, I can tell you that the rule in delivery system selection is to *select the most readily available and economical items that will provide the features called for by your objectives.* If you don't have any objectives, you'll be easy pickins for those who want to sell you more media hardware than you need. (Watch out for people who come to you with the direction, "We need you to do a video," or whatever the delivery system of the day is.)

> **NOTE:** A common error is to decide on a delivery system for a course, rather than for a single objective or module. This is an error because a *course* could easily consist of pieces that could be learned by computer or other "distance learning" method in combination with one or more classroom pieces where instructor support is available. The mistake is to think that a course has to be delivered by one medium or another, rather than by a *delivery system* consisting of a combination of methods and media.

How to Do It

Complete the following steps for each of your objectives. Believe me when I say it won't take long.

1. List the things that will be needed in order to provide relevant practice of the objective. To do this you would look at the things you listed while describing relevant practice requirements. Underline or circle the items that are *things* (e.g., disassembled crankshaft, drill press, computer keyboard, tool kit, head of hair).

2. Check that the items selected for practice are those that will allow students to make the most responses (get the most practice) per unit of time.

3. Then, if you have other items on the list, decide how you will provide them. For example, if your list says, "List of examples," or "Descriptions of problem situations," write a word or two beside it to say how you will present these items. Will the examples be presented in print? If so, what's the most convenient way to present that print? On paper? On film? On a video or computer screen? If your list says you need a person to assist with the practice, write who that person will be. A student? You? Someone else?

4. If the module will require content in addition to practice, review your content summary and say how you will present the content. Pick something that has the feature needed for the content involved.

5. Now think about your target population. Are the items you selected appropriate for them? If not, select something else with similar features. For example, if you have decided to present information in print but your audience can't read too well, pick a way to present the information that demands less reading.

6. Are the items you've listed available to you? If not, select something that is.

7. Are the items you selected easy for students to use, easy for them to get, and easy for them to operate? If not, try to find something more practical.

8. Finally, can you think of items that will give you the feature you need but that are less expensive to buy and to maintain? If so, change your original selection. For example, although you initially decided to present information by computer, second thought may convince you that a series of explained photos placed in a binder would be cheaper to produce and easier to maintain.

And that's it. Sure, there are times when a decision can be a little trickier to make, as when students to be trained are scattered around the world. But most of the time it will be a simple matter of selecting the things you will need (1) to provide relevant practice and feedback and (2) to present information, demonstrations, and examples. Try not to make it harder than it is.

Example #1:   **TPop:**   Machinist apprentices

Objective: On a metal lathe, be able to turn brass round stock to blueprint specifications.

Relevant Practice Description: Practice will require a lathe, brass round stock, blueprints. Feedback by instructor or assistant.

Delivery System: Metal lathe, brass round stock, blueprints, instructor or assistant. Micrometer for measuring finished practice work. Instructor to present content (to minimize reading load), supervise practice, and provide feedback.

Example #2:   **TPop:**   Instructional technology students

Objective: Given any objective, be able to prepare a skill check item to match that objective. Criteria: Each item calls for (a) the performance stated in the objective, under (b) the conditions described by the objective.

Relevant Practice Description: Students will be given objectives and asked to write test items. Feedback: model of correct or acceptable items; checklist of key features.

Delivery System: Sample objectives, checklist, and instruction presented in print.

Example #3:   **TPop:**   Sales trainees

Objective: Given product information and the product, be able to describe all key features and benefits to a customer. Criteria: All information presented is factually correct, and customer is not insulted or humiliated.

Relevant Practice Description: In private, another student will role-play a customer and the trainee will use product information and the product itself to practice describing features and benefits. The session will be videotaped. Feedback: Student and instructor will view tape while applying a checklist of criteria.

Delivery System: A student to role-play a customer; videotaping and playback equipment; product information in print; the product itself; instructor to provide information and feedback.

Example #4:   **TPop:**   Medical students

Objective: Given a functioning computer terminal with the Medical Information System application installed and running, be able to enter medical records and orders. Criteria: All entered data are correct and assigned to the correct patient.

Relevant Practice Description: In private, students will practice entering data into a computer terminal.

Delivery System: A computer terminal loaded with the MIS application system; sample records and data. Feedback to be provided by computer.

To Learn More: See Resources #4, #15, and #20.

15
Module Drafting

Situation: You have all your analysis documents, and you know what will be needed to provide students with practice. You are ready to draft instruction.

Once you have your TPop. description, objectives, relevant practice description, and content summary, your module will practically write itself. Well, all right, maybe that's a slight exaggeration, but not much. Think about it. Every module includes an objective, a skill check description, a description of relevance, practice, and feedback. You've already got those components, with the exception of the description of relevance. So you're almost ready to draft. True, instruction is as much art as science, but the components you already have will take a lot of the guesswork out of module drafting.

How It Goes

The way you actually put pencil to paper (or fingers to keyboard) when drafting a module will depend mainly on how the instruction will be delivered to the students. For example, if the instruction will be delivered by audio tape, you would draft the module in the form of a script. If it will be delivered

Figure 15.1 Basic Module Floor Plan

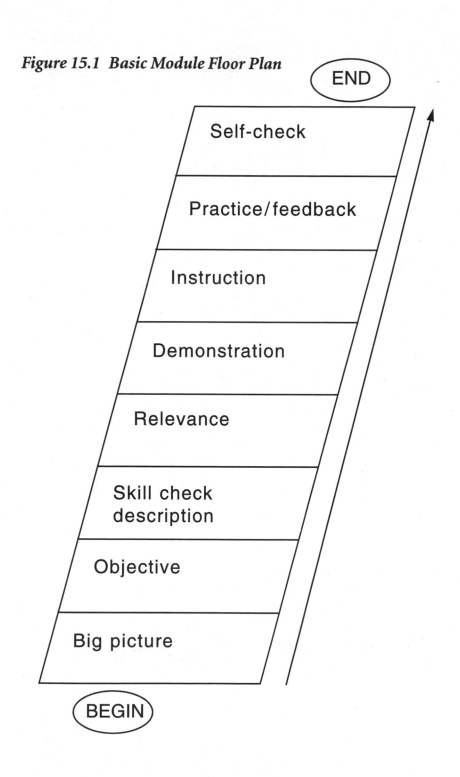

in print, you would write the instruction in a form intended to be read by students. If it will be delivered by computer, you will draft the individual screens that will be viewed by the students. If you will be the primary medium through which much of your instruction will be presented, you will most likely draft the module in the form of a lesson plan. But no matter how the instruction will ultimately be delivered, it begins with words on paper or screen.

The Floor Plan

Whether stated or not, every lesson or module has a floor plan. Something happens first, then something else happens, followed by something else. (How's that for profound?) The kind of floor plan you should be aiming for is one that includes the following components, in approximately the order shown in Figure 15.1.

Big picture: Reminds or shows students where they are in the larger scheme of the course. (Always included.)

Objective: Shows them the objective they are to accomplish, in terms they can understand. (Always included.)

Skill check description: Describes what students will have to do to demonstrate mastery of the objective.

Relevance: Explains and/or demonstrates why the accomplishment of this objective is important to *them*. (Always included.)

Demo: Shows what students will look like when performing the objective. (As needed.)

Instruction: Teaches students what they need to know before they can practice the objective. (As needed.)

Practice/feedback: Provides practice in the objective, along with timely information about performance and progress. (Always included.)

Self-check: Provides students a way to check whether they are ready to demonstrate their ability to perform as the objective requires. (As needed.)

NOTE: The skill check is not listed here as it is not contained in the body of the module.

Notice that the floor plan is not media specific; that is, it can be followed no matter who or what presents the instruction. No matter how the instruction is delivered, students should know at all times why they are doing what they're doing and how to tell when they're doing it satisfactorily, and they should be afforded an opportunity to practice until they *can* perform as desired.

Different lessons will have somewhat different floor plans, simply because the objectives are different and need different module components to accomplish them. Where one module will contain nothing but practice and feedback, another will have considerable guided presentation with information, examples, and demonstrations. Where one can be self-paced, another will need to be group-paced.

The goal is to let students in on the secret of what they will be expected to do, teach them whatever they need to know before they can practice the objective, provide practice and feedback, and then offer a skill check that will assess whether the objective has been accomplished. Use whatever combination of module components are needed to get you there.

Using Existing Material

It is a waste of time to "reinvent the wheel," so save time by locating existing material that can be used as part or all of the instruction. If it already exists, save your time and use it.

But use only those portions that are relevant to accomplishing the objectives. If you make students sit through an entire 30-minute video, for example, when only 3 minutes of it are relevant to the objective, you're not only wasting their time, you're squandering their motivation to learn. The same is true if you make them read an entire chapter of text when only one page will help accomplish an objective. The object is to locate potentially useful material and identify those pieces that will be directly useful in helping someone toward an objective.

When potentially useful materials include a textbook, you will seldom need to include the entire text. Textbooks are written in a sequence that makes sense to the author, or in a sequence that offers a "logical" presentation of the subject matter. They are seldom written in a sequence that is logical from the students' point of view. Further, they always contain a good deal more content than is needed to accomplish the objectives you have on hand. Therefore, when a textbook includes material useful for accomplishing one or more objectives, portions of that text will usually be used in a sequence other than the one in which it was written.

This is not a problem, of course, except when an accrediting agency wants to know why you are using the text "out of sequence" or not using a text at all. If your objectives have been derived from a good analysis, however, you will be able to show the rationale that caused you to select the content that you did. "Or," said one of the kindly souls who helped test the manuscript for this book, "you can always send them an 'approved' course outline and teach another."

How to Do It

Here are some suggestions about how to draft your modules:

1. Review the items on your relevant practice description, along with the module objective.

2. Locate existing instructional materials that might be useful, and compare them with the objective of the module they will be intended for. Mark those pieces or passages that will be relevant. Put the name or number of the objective on the appropriate passage (you should be able to associate each instructional action with the objective it is intended to accomplish).

3. Begin by writing the objective itself as it will be presented to the students; i.e., use language the students will understand at this point in their development.

4. Write the practice/feedback section (the back end) of the module. Say where students should get the practice equipment (if any) or other practice items they will need; tell them what to do with these things, and tell them how to evaluate their practice performance.

5. Write a description or describe a demonstration that will show why it is important *to the student* to develop the competence described by the objective. Remind students of where this objective fits into the larger scheme of things. (Note: Sometimes the importance of the objective is so obvious that little or nothing need be done here. You can't make a dead horse deader by beating it.)

6. If you will need to instruct before students will be ready to practice, and if you will be presenting the instruction

mainly by lecture, draft a lesson plan. Outline the content you will present in one column, and say what students will be doing in another column. List the examples you will use and any practice items that will be needed to teach students how to recognize competent performance of the objective. Make sure that students are active (doing something other than listening or taking notes) during at least two-thirds of the instructional period.

7. Regardless of the delivery system used to present the instruction to the students, be sure to include the directions that will tell them what to do. Include directions such as:

- View videotape V-34.

- Check your answers on the next page.

- Click on the best response.

- Have an instructor review your findings.

- Read pages _____ before practicing.

- Get the performance check and do what it says.

- Ask an instructor to set up the equipment so that you can demonstrate your mastery of the objective.

- When you need an instructor, click on the black icon.

- Complete the following practice exercise.

- Ask another student to fill out Checksheet W as you conduct the practice interview.

- Ask a student to role-play a customer as you practice the selling skill.

- Complete pages 5-8 in the workbook.

- Ask an instructor to demonstrate _____.

- Give your practice videotape to an instructor for review.

- Sign up for the group practice session.

- Sign up for the brazing demonstration.

In other words, make sure that the module directs the student to the instructional sources and to the practice. When few instructional resources exist, they will either have to be created and included in the module or presented by you. In the latter case the module would indicate to students when they should be ready for your instruction on the topic being studied.

8. Finally, write what students should do to demonstrate their achievement of the objective. If this will be in the form of a written test, tell them where to get it and how it will be administered. If a demonstration of skill on a machine or with a process is in order, tell them where to go and what to get. In other words, state what they will have to do to be eligible to begin another module.

If You're Stuck

Sometimes our pencils go limp or our brains turn to mush. In other words, sometimes we get stuck. Fortunately, there is a simple solution. Write the practice section of the module first.

You already have a description of relevant practice, so drafting the practice section should be easy and help get you started. Say what equipment and supplies students will have to get, say where to get them and what to do with them, and describe how feedback will be made available. Once you've done that, you will have a much clearer picture of what the remainder of the module should be like.

To be perfectly honest, you might consider writing the practice section first for all the modules you develop. Here's why: Just as the writing of a criterion test item is a good way to find out where the objectives need sharpening, writing the practice section is a good way to sharpen your understanding of what else, if anything, will need to be added to the module in the way of content. Just as the result (the objective) tells you what kind of practice you need, the practice will suggest the additional content you will need.

The Lesson Plan

A lesson plan is an instructional prescription, a blueprint describing the activities the instructor and student may engage in to reach the objectives of the course. Its main purpose is to prescribe the key events that should occur during the module. If the instructor finds it necessary to deliver most or all of the instruction through lectures, the lesson plan is the guide to the instructor's actions. When a module is put into the hands of the student, it performs a similar function: it tells the student what to do, where to locate the instructional resources, how to practice, and how to demonstrate competence when ready.

The precise format of the lesson plan is less important than making sure it performs its important functions. As you have already listed or summarized the content of each lesson, the task of preparing a module will be relatively simple. Whatever the format used, however, make sure it emphasizes what *students* will be doing rather than what the instructor will be doing. That way you won't be likely to fall into the trap of developing a course principally on the basis of what you *like* to do rather than on the basis of what students need to do to accomplish the objectives.

Example #1: **Hairstyling.** This example is a module written in the form of a lesson plan for use by someone delivering the instruction by lecturing.

Objective: Using hair-shaping implements and supplies, be able to cut the client's hair to the requested hairstyle.

Instructor Activity	Student Activity
1. Explain purpose of the skill and when it is used. Describe objective and hairstyles to be learned. Describe skill check.	
2. Demonstrate use of each hairstyling tool.	
3. Hold up hairstying tools and ask students to name each.	Respond with names of tools. Ask questions during demo.
4. Demonstrate and explain first hairstyle.	Ask questions during demo. Students practice on each other.
5. Explain and illustrate common errors and how they are avoided.	
6. Correct student errors.	
7. Demonstrate and explain second hairstyle.	Ask questions during demo.
8. Correct student errors.	Students practice on each other.
9. Describe common errors and how to avoid or correct them on second hairstyle.	Students ask questions.
10. Initiate individual performance test.	Students claiming to be ready are tested first, while others continue practicing.
(Continue with additional hairstyles, if any.)	

Sometimes it may be appropriate to add an "Equipment and Materials" list somewhere in the lesson plan. This will provide a ready checklist of the items that will be needed for completing the lesson. Some instructors prefer to add this list near the top of their lesson plans, while others prefer to add a third column to the lesson plan itself. This third column is used as space in which to list items (things) needed for each of the lesson components.

The main thing to keep in mind in lesson planning is to adopt a format that will help you rather than get in your way. And remember: There is no *instructional* reason why all your lesson plans should look alike. Though you may have a bureaucratic mandate to adopt a particular format, you can always fulfill that requirement and then build a lesson plan in a format that will help you *and* meet the needs of the objectives to be taught.

Examples #2 and #3

The next two examples are from a criterion-referenced module (i.e., instruction is designed to accomplish specified objectives). The first may be partly self-paced; the second is entirely self-paced. The module was borrowed from the nine-module course entitled "Instructional Module Development," by R. F. Mager. It is intended for the population of students learning how to be instructional developers and shows them how to prepare the instructions that will be needed when their course will be taught by someone *other than themselves*.

Example #2: Prepare Implementation Instructions.

This example shows the module in lesson-plan format for use by someone delivering the instruction by lecture.

Objective: Given a module of instruction that accomplishes its objective, be able to prepare the directions and instructions that will enable the module to work when administered by another instructor.

Instructor Activity	Student Activity
1. Explain importance of the activity.	
2. Hand out example module.	Read example module. List information needed in preparation for teaching the sample module.
3. Ask students to list the items and information they feel they would need before they could teach the sample module.	
4. Ask students to volunteer the information on their lists, and ask other students to add items or to comment.	Discuss the lists.
5. Hand out Implementation Checklist. Answer questions about the items.	Ask questions.
6. Ask each student to draft the implementation items and instructions needed by another instructor expecting to teach the module.	Write implementation material.
7. Have student give his or her module and implementation instructions to another student. Ask student to list missing items.	Review someone else's module and implementation material and list missing items.
8. Discuss results of the practice.	
9. Administer criterion test.	Prepare implementation material for a second module the student has already drafted.

Example #3: Prepare Implementation Instructions.

Here is the same module as in Example #2, but written in a form to be handed to students who are working through a criterion-referenced, self-paced course in which they are learning to develop modules for similarly conducted courses. In these courses students work at their own pace until they can demonstrate achievement of an objective, and then they move on to the next module.

As you read through the module, see if you can identify the following components (remembering that the skill check itself is not part of the body of the module):

- Objective

- Criterion test description

- Description of relevance

- "Prepare to practice" content

- Practice

- Source of feedback for the practice

- Directions to the student

- Job aid to guide performance

Here is the module in its entirety:

Module: Prepare Implementation Instructions.

Objective: Given a module of instruction that accomplishes its objective, be able to prepare the directions and instructions that will enable the module to work when administered by another instructor.

Criteria: The directions and instructions answer questions about (a) what to collect in the way of materials, supplies, equipment, resources; (b) how to prepare the equipment, materials, and space for use; (c) how to answer common questions and handle common problems; (d) how and when to suggest alternative resources and activities, if any; and (e) how to review performance.

Skill Check: To demonstrate your competence, you will be asked to prepare the directions and instructions that would be needed to allow your module to be administered by someone else. You will be asked to: Locate two participants willing to assist, give one of them your module and additional materials, and ask him/her to serve as instructor. Ask the other to serve as student. You'll observe the session (without interrupting) and make notes of any assistance you need to offer to make the session work.

(**NOTE:** Here's where the instruction for this module begins.)

Why Are Implementation Instructions Important?

The most terrific and fantastic machine in the whole world is useless unless someone knows how to operate it. Unless someone knows what to do with it, it will just sit there gathering dust. Worse, without good operating instructions, people

Example #3, continued:

are likely to misuse those wonderful devices. They may even damage themselves or others in the process.

Modules of instruction are like that. It's one thing to make them work while they are under *your* control. It's something else to be able to make them work when they are under *someone else's* control. It's one thing for you to be able to smooth the path of the learner by offering a resource here or by anticipating a problem there. It's something else to be able to get others to do likewise.

You have done the first part . . . the big part; you've created modules. You've tested them and revised them and you've made them work. Now it's time to add whatever is needed so that someone else can make them work. And if there is one thing you can believe, it's this: Murphy's Law lives; if anything can go wrong, it will. People will administer your module at the wrong time, in the wrong way, without providing the necessary materials or supplies or space. But it's even worse than that. Unless you provide instructors with all the information they need to implement the module correctly, they won't administer it incorrectly . . . *they won't use it at all.* It will go right up on the shelf. After all, the instructor "knows" how to teach the material in your module, and since that way is familiar, it will take precedence over your module . . . unless you make the process of module administration clear and complete, put the words into their mouths that they will say to their students, and tell them exactly what they need to do to prepare and to administer the module.

But what else is there, you may be wondering? After all, you have created modules that are self-contained in that they only need an instructor to provide feedback for practice. What else is there? Think about it this way.

Example #3, continued:

The Slot in the Wall

Imagine that you will slip your module through a slot in the wall, to be administered by an instructor on the other side. You can peek through a little window to see what is happening, but you can neither talk to the instructor nor use body language to signal what should be done next. All you can do is to slip your package through the wall and watch.

What would happen? The instructor picks up the package and fingers through the pieces. What will he or she do then? Would this instructor know whether there are some preparations that need to be made before giving the module to a student? How would this instructor know what to read or look at first? Would this person know:

- what to collect in the way of equipment, supplies and materials, or resources?

- what sort of environment to arrange?

- how to prepare equipment for practice?

- how to schedule students for practice on scarce equipment or other resources?

- how to anticipate and handle common problems or questions?

- how to review practice exercises, if any?

- how to review skill check performance?

- when and how to suggest alternative resources and activities?

Example #3, continued:

If the answer to any of these questions is "No," then something is missing and needs to be added. Usually, this will consist of a "Note to Course Manager" in the self-evaluation material or in the Course Manager Manual. Sometimes it will mean drafting a list of supplies that need to be collected. When students will have to be scheduled for time on equipment or for use of a room, it may mean drafting a sign-up sheet or informing instructors on how the scheduling should be done and how it should be used. And unless you prepare and provide the answers to the above questions, you should expect that your module will be laid aside rather than used as you intend.

You see, you are now dealing with a target population different from the one for which your module was created. You are dealing with the audience of instructors, rather than of students. You are now trying to package your module in such a way that the instructor population will know how to implement the instruction you created for your student population. Quite a different matter from "packaging" a module that will teach an objective. It's the difference between creating a highly flexible computer and creating the instructions that will allow someone to use it. It's the difference between creating a gourmet dinner and creating the recipe that will enable others to re-create that same gourmet dinner. It's the difference between creating a fantastic jazz solo and writing the sheet music that will cause others to play it the same way you do.

So to make your module usable by others, it will need to be accompanied by whatever directions/instructions that will allow others to follow the same implementation steps that you do. And those instructions and directions will need to be just as specific as you can make them. If you are writing instructions for a role-play, for example, rather than simply suggest that the instructor "Give the participants a little pep talk to get

Example #3, continued:

them in the mood," tell them exactly what to say. Put the words right in their mouths.

"Say to the participants the following . . ." Whenever you have to provide directions or instructions for someone else to give to students, be as precise as you can.

Here's an example:

For the Instructor:

1. Get the practice envelope marked R-1, and check to see that it contains the five drawings labeled 1 through 5.

2. Set the controls on the white print machine to accept a medium-density drawing.

3. Hand the envelope to the student, and say to the student: "Here are five typical jobs to be run on your white print machine. Tell me how you would set up the machine to run ten copies of each drawing."

4. Write the student's response in the space provided on the response sheet.

5. If the student's response for the first drawing is correct, say "Good." If it is not correct, tell him or her what the correct response is. (This is a practice session, not a test.)

6. Provide this type of feedback as each item is completed.

Though you may not have to do this sort of thing often, when you do, be precise. Before drafting your own implementation material, it will be useful to look at a few other examples.

Example #3, continued:

Here Is What to Do

1. Ask the course manager to lend you a copy of the *Course Manager Manual* booklet for this course.

2. Review the table of contents to note the types of information contained in the manual.

3. Read the section labeled "Module Notes." Note the types of information and comments included there.

4. Review your own *Course Control Documents* booklet. What type of information included there would help an instructor to administer your module?

5. Borrow the module of a colleague who is also working through this course. Pretend that you will be teaching that module as part of your own course. List the types of additional information that you would want to have before administering the module to a group of students in *your* learning environment.

6. If you have followed the steps described above, you should be ready to tackle the instructor directions for your own module. It may be easier to do if you break the task into four sections and deal with them one at a time.

    a. *Materials Collection*

    In a large number of instances, a module will simply need to be made available to students; not only is the module self-contained, but all the items needed to

Example #3, continued:

make the module function are enclosed within it. Others require the use of equipment or materials or resources. Someone has to be directed to collect these items before the module can be used.

Is everything the student will need contained within the module itself, within the package of print or tapes or disks you have drafted?

Does the student need to use something, fix something, adjust something, fill out something? List those some-things as the items that will need to be collected before the module can be attempted.

b. *Preparation*

If you only have one Limpmobile for each ten students, and if each student has to practice replacing the In-law Ejector, someone is going to have to schedule the prac-tice time. Can it be accomplished by a simple sign-up sheet hung on a door or wall? Will another method be needed? However it is to be accomplished, an instructor or someone will have to prepare the mechanism by which the practice will be scheduled.

Will students need to fill out forms? Will they need to travel to where the equipment they are learning about is located? If so, where will the forms be placed? How will students get to the equipment location?

Will students be expected to practice troubleshooting equipment? If so, what kind of practice "bugs" (troubles) should the instructor insert? In what order? Clear direc-tions will need to be prepared for the instructor prepar-ing to administer the module.

Example #3, continued:

c. *Implementation*

Sometimes the instructor will have a role to play while the module is being attempted by a student. It may be that the course manager will be expected to review a practice exercise or perhaps to demonstrate a procedure. If so, the course manager should be prepared for these activities; instruction on how to handle these activities should be made available.

Are there typical questions that students will ask, common problems to watch out for? Are there typical errors during practice? If so, draft some comments designed to help the course manager implement the module the way you would like to have it implemented.

d. *Evaluation*

When a skill check involves responding to a number of questions for which there are right or wrong answers, students are encouraged to compare their responses with those that are contained in the self-evaluation materials. But what about all those instances in which a skill check asks for original or creative responses or asks students to write something, draft something, make something, say something? The course manager will be expected to review the work and to determine whether the performance is OK or not yet OK and provide diagnostic, and perhaps corrective, feedback.

The skill check for this module, for example, asks you to prepare the directions and instructions that may be needed to implement your module and to take that material along with your module to a course manager for review. Two things have been done to prepare the course manager to handle this review: (1) A Module Note in

Example #3, continued:

the *Course Manager Manual* describes the activity and offers hints in handling typical omissions; (2) A checklist of items to look for is included in the self-evaluation material.

Do you have self-evaluation material written for your skill check? Is it self-explanatory, or would a course manager benefit from some directions or comments from you about how to proceed?

Your Turn

If you have followed the instructions on the previous pages, you should be ready for the Skill. It will ask you to prepare the items that will be needed before the module can be implemented by someone other than yourself. You will be expected to hand your module and the instructions to a colleague, who will in turn be expected to administer the module successfully to another workshop participant . . . *without help from you.* Use the *Module Implementation Checklist* as a guide.

Module Implementation Checklist

1. If materials are used in the module, is there a materials list for the course manager?

2. Are there instructions on how materials should be set out or prepared for use?

3. If equipment is involved, are there instructions about how to locate and set up the equipment?

4. If troubleshooting practice is involved, are there instructions on exactly what practice troubles to use and in what order? Are there instructions on how to set up the practice session?

Example #3, continued:

5. If equipment or space must be shared, is there information on how to schedule the time?

6. Is there information on how to handle common questions or problems?

7. Are there directions on how to handle practice exercises?

8. Is there information about how and when to suggest the use of alternate resources and activities?

9. Are there suggestions on how to review criterion test performance?

This was an admittedly long example, but I feel that you deserve to see what a complete example of a criterion-referenced module might look like. Other such modules may be presented by different combinations of media, but all would contain the necessary module components.

You should now have all the knowledge you need to use the Module Checklist on the next page.

MODULE CHECKLIST

Use this checklist to assure that your modules include all the components they need for facilitating the performance you want.

<u>DOES THE MODULE:</u>

1. Have a title or label?   _____

2. Show the student the objective in terms   _____
   he or she can understand?

3. Describe what the student will have to do   _____
   to demonstrate competence?

4. Describe or illustrate the place or relevance   _____
   of the objective in the larger scheme of things
   (if needed)? From the student's point of view?

5. Demonstrate or show what the student will   _____
   be like when performing the objective (if
   demonstration is needed)?

6. Prepare the student to practice?   _____

7. Include relevant practice of the objective?   _____

8. Provide the tools, items, objects needed   _____
   for relevant practice?

9. Provide relevant feedback for the practice?   _____

10. Practice what it teaches? Is it free of modeling   _____
    errors?

11. Show trainees exactly what to do or where to   _____
    go at each point in the module? i.e., are there
    adequate directions?

12. Help trainees decide when they are ready to   _____
    demonstrate their competence?

13. Use the simplest possible delivery system?   _____

14. Flow from beginning to end? Does it have   _____
    continuity?

15. Contain no unnecessary obstacles between   _____
    the student and the learning?

16. Have a criterion test and associated   _____
    self-evaluation (feedback)?

If you follow the how-to-do-it steps described in this chapter, you will find the job of drafting your instruction greatly simplified.

NOTE: This procedure will in no way restrict your ability to make your instruction interesting and motivating. On the contrary, students always seem more interested in instruction they perceive as being relevant to their needs or desires. So don't be concerned that "lean" development will take the heart out of the instruction. No matter how tight you make your instruction, there will always be some slack in it for transitions, extra examples, war stories, humor, and anecdotes. But with properly constructed instruction, you will always know that no matter how much or how little you embellish, the instruction will do what it is supposed to do.

To make your instruction work, make sure you teach things not yet known, provide the instruction needed to get students ready to practice the objective, provide practice and feedback, and then take steps to find out whether the student can perform as desired.

To Learn More: See Resource #16.

16
Tryout

Situation: Modules are in the process of being drafted or have already been drafted. You want to know how well they work and what to do to improve them.

Unless you've got a license in mind reading, tryout is the touchstone to instructional success. Oh, sure, I know there isn't time for "that sort of thing." I know that lead times are usually short and instructors don't have much time for course development. But that doesn't change the fact that tryout is the key to success. I know you would agree with me if I were talking about products other than instruction—in many instances you wouldn't even touch the product if you thought it *didn't* go through tryout.

"Has this airplane been tested?"

"What?"

"Has this plane gone through tryouts to make sure it works?"

"We don't have time for that. We consider the maiden flights the tryouts."

"Oh."

Or,

"Has this medicine been through clinical testing?"

"What?"

"Has this medicine been tested on humans?"

"No need for that. We'll know it works if nobody dies from it."

"Oh."

You see the point. No matter how good we are at instructional development, we still don't know for sure whether, or how well, the instruction will work until we try it out. If there is no time for a tryout before a full class of students shuffles in, then the maiden course will have to be considered the tryout. But don't set the materials in concrete until the results of at least one tryout are in. Make only enough copies of things to take you through the first cycle. Believe me, you will want to fix some things before anyone else sees or experiences it. I'd rather have the errors and opportunities for improvement pointed out *before* "going public" rather than after, wouldn't you? Wouldn't you like to know what the critic will say *before* opening night, rather than after—so you can have a chance to smooth out the lumps?

How to Do It

You already know how to conduct a course, so there's little to learn before being ready to conduct a tryout. The main thing you need to know is that the answers to your tryout questions are readily available. Whatever you may want to know about how well your module is working or how well it fits your audience, your students will be your best source of information. And why not? The instruction is being developed for their benefit, so they should be consulted on how well the job has been done.

After all, when your physician whacks you on the back and asks, "Did that hurt?" he or she is asking you for information. When a shoe salesclerk asks you how the fit feels, information from the customer is being requested. So be sure to include your students as the key source of information about how well the instruction fits and about how well it works.

There are two kinds of tryout. The first is a check of the individual module or lesson plan during the development process. It involves trying it out on one person at a time, until all the major kinks have been removed. The second is a tryout of the entire course. Here's how.

For Self-Paced Courses

Try out each module on at least one person before you test the entire course. Find someone (*one* person at a time; if you use large samples at this point, you'll be wasting your time and theirs) as close to your target population as possible. If a member of your target population is available, fine. But it isn't necessary. As long as you find someone similar to your TPop. who cannot perform the objective, that person will be a big help. But do a tryout even if the person most available cannot understand the technical language of the module or doesn't fit the TPop. in other ways. That individual will still locate oversights and errors that you will want to correct before you let anyone else see your work. Here are the steps:

1. Locate someone who is willing to work through the module. (We will refer to this person as the "tester.")

2. Write out your instructions to that person. Explain that this is a test of the instruction rather than of the person, and that you are looking for ways to improve the module. Explain that he or she should make a mark on any part of the material that is difficult or that is a turnoff, or that is bothersome for any other reason. If the material is being presented by a computer or other device, or by an instructor, ask students to make notes (on the pad you provide) of their comments as they go.

3. Let the person read the instructions, and answer any questions that might arise.

4. Give him or her the materials, show where things are located (if appropriate), and then back away.

5. Sit in the corner and *do not interfere* with the tryout. Don't do anything that might be distracting, such as practice your golf swing or tap your pencil. Do not offer information when you see that the tester is in trouble. Instead, make a note on your pad.

6. If you are asked a question, answer it and then *make a note of it*. Always make a note about the reason for your interventions. These notes will tell you what you will need to do to smooth out the instruction. If the tester turns to you and asks a question, one of my colleagues suggests saying, "Do what you think the module is telling you to do," and then noting what he/she does.

7. When the tryout is over, *listen* to the comments of the tester. You can always ignore the suggestions if you choose; you cannot ignore suggestions you don't have.

8. When the tryout is finished, thank the tester profusely, and be sure to add the tester's name to the list of those who helped in shaping the instruction. Be sure to spell the name correctly.

For Instructor-Led Courses

If yours is mainly an instructor-led (lecture-driven) course, the tryout pattern is somewhat different.

1. Find a colleague willing to help.

2. Ask the colleague to compare each of your lesson plans to its objective and answer the following questions:

   a. Will students be shown the module objective in terms they will understand?

   b. Will the importance of the module be explained or demonstrated?

   c. Is practice offered in the objective? Is feedback offered?

   d. Does there appear to be more content than needed? Less? About the right amount?

   e. Will students be doing something other than listening to the instructor for more than 50 percent of the time?

Notice that this procedure does not ask your colleague to dictate or in any way interfere with your style or method of instruction. It merely provides an external pair of eyes that will help you to spot the holes you may have missed while putting the modules together.

Technical Review

It is always helpful to have a colleague or two look through the material to make sure there are no technical errors. If you really need help with the technical accuracy, you might consider a colleague review before the module tryout. If you are the technical expert and just want to make sure you haven't made any big boo-boos, then do it after the tryout. The procedure is the same as that described above for the self-paced course, except that you would not need to watch the review. You would hand, or send, the materials to the colleague along with appropriate instructions and request for assistance. And you would be certain to follow Step 8 in the previous instructions (i.e., thank profusely and record the person's name, correctly spelled).

Caution #1: Though asked for comments on technical accuracy, your colleague may feel compelled to make comments on your instructional approach: "That's not the way I teach"; "It's never been done that way"; "You've left out some of the theory." Your response should be to smile, thank the individual for the assistance, and then feel free to ignore all but those comments that relate to technical accuracy.

Course Tryout

When each of the modules has been tried out at least once and revised on the basis of the information collected, and you have sequenced the individual lessons into a course, you will be ready for a full-course tryout. Here's how.

1. Collect all the things you will need to conduct the course. Refer to the modules; they should each begin with a list of the items required for the instruction. If you don't have everything you need and that you think is reasonable to expect, or that you were counting on, use

the professional approach to procurement: Hold your breath, throw a tantrum, throw yourself at the feet of your department head or manager, and plead for the items you need. If you're in the military, the term "midnight requisitioning" may be appropriate here.

2. Duplicate enough materials for the first run-through. Not more. Get a large stamp that says DRAFT and stamp all the materials.

3. If other instructors or assistants will participate in the tryout, walk them through the procedures. If they are going to assist with the instruction itself, give them some practice in handling the portions they will be assigned.

4. Make a copy of the course procedures (described in Chapter 18) for each student.

5. Put everything in its place, and then check your preparation.

6. Get a notebook (five by eight inches or larger) and in big letters write on it, "Comments and Suggestions."

7. Place this book in a prominent place in the classroom (your desk is fine for this).

8. When the students arrive, welcome them, tell them which course this is (in case they thought they were waiting for a bus to Fresno), hand out copies of the course procedures, and explain them briefly.

9. Tell them that this is an update of an existing course, or a new course, whichever is true. Then tell them that you are sincerely asking their help in improving it. If it's an update, assure them that what they're getting is at least as

good as it used to be. Show them the comments book and encourage them to write their comments in it. If they make suggestions directly to you during the course, thank them and then suggest they write in the notebook. They will feel more rewarded for daring to make a suggestion.

10. Conduct the course—according to the procedures you have given the students.

11. If the course is more than one day long, and more than one instructor is conducting the course, schedule end-of-day debriefing sessions.

12. When it is over, review the comments in the notebook, along with the notes you made yourself.

13. Make the indicated revisions. If there were a lot of revisions, then consider the next cycle a second tryout and repeat the procedure. Go to press only when the indicated revisions are minor or cosmetic in nature, rather than substantive.

14. Provide feedback to those who helped with the tryout(s). When possible, give each an autographed copy of the final product (or at least some part of it).

Cosmetic vs. Substantive Comments

What's the difference between cosmetic and substantive revisions? *Substantive* comments suggest changes to the content or the sequence of the content. Suggestions that you should move this chapter from here to there, or to delete unneeded material, or that you correct technical errors, are suggestions to make substantive changes. Keep testing until the number of substantive comments drops to zero.

Cosmetic comments refer to style. When testers pick at your choice of words, or at your manner of writing, or your "political correctness," you are hearing comments about the cosmetics of your course. These are comments you may or may not want to do something about.

One mark of the professional is the insistence on tryouts before "going public." Just as plays are tried out off-Broadway, night-club acts polished in the smaller lounges, and products tested until they meet specifications, instruction (as well as job aids, questionnaires, and surveys) is put through tryout before being considered ready for regular consumption. The time you spend on tryout is time you will never regret.

To Learn More: See Resource #16.

17
Sequencing

Situation: Modules have been drafted, and you want to determine the most efficient sequence in which they should be devoured by your students.

Since not everything can be learned at once, instruction must be offered in some sort of sequence. One thing must come before another. How shall we decide on the order in which the students should address the individual lessons? By trying to determine what the most beneficial sequence of events would be from the *student's* point of view.

Sequence and Order

It would be useful to begin by considering the nature of sequence and order. Think about it this way. Imagine yourself sitting at a table that has a box of children's blocks on it. Your task is to make a single stack of blocks. Obviously, you must place them one at a time; first you must put down one block, then you set another one on top of it, and so on. But you don't necessarily have to pile them in any order. As long as one block is on top of another, it doesn't matter which block comes before some other block.

If, on the other hand, you were asked to pile them up alphabetically, then the order in which you piled them *would* matter. You'd have to put down the A before the B, and the B before the C.

So What?

What does this have to do with instructional sequencing? Just this. There is always a sequence of lessons; that is, one lesson always follows another. But there doesn't always have to be a *prescribed* order; that is, they don't always have to be studied in the same sequence by each and every student. To understand this point, look back to the example skill hierarchy in Chapter 8. Notice how many of the skills are independent of one another—that is, shown side by side. Though all of these skills must be learned before the terminal objective (the one at the top) can be practiced, the *order* in which they are learned doesn't matter—any one of them could be productively learned before any of the others is attempted. And when the order doesn't matter, it is better to let the students decide on the sequence in which they will do the learning. Having some control helps their motivation to learn.

Traditionally, the only guidelines for sequencing instructional activities have been, "Teach your lessons in a logical sequence," and "Teach from the simple to the complex." That's about as helpful as telling someone to "be good." Those rules are just too vague and have too many possible meanings. After all, *everyone* believes they teach in a logical sequence. But if you look to see what they are in fact doing, you will find that some use a historical sequence, teaching that which happened first, what happened next, and so on. Others teach "theory" before practice. Others claim to teach from the simple to the complex, but usually use a sequence that is opposite to the one they would use if guided by the *students'* definition of simple to complex. And so on.

Fortunately, we can now take most of the guesswork out of sequencing. Here's how.

How to Do It

The goals are to inflame the students' interest in the subject, keep their motivation high, and make sure they have accomplished the course objectives by the time they leave.

1. Begin the course with the topic of highest interest to the students, regardless of where the full treatment of that topic falls within the course. For example, imagine you have signed up for a course in locksmithing because you want to learn to pick locks like the detectives on TV. You show up for the course ready and eager to get started. You sandpaper your fingertips and get ready to pick your first lock. But the first week is on the history of locksmithing, the second covers the theory of locks, and the third is on assembly and disassembly. By then there are cobwebs under your armpits, mildew on your brain, and you're wondering why you came.

   No matter what the item of highest interest to your students may be, begin there. Jerk them into the course by giving them a taste of the goodies. (As one of the testers of this book remarked, "A picture is worth a thousand words; an experience is worth a thousand pictures.") Spend at least half an hour on that topic, and let them know that there will be more about it later. Then, try to sprinkle the items of high student interest throughout the course.

One instructor I talked with recently couldn't understand why students were uneasy with his course at the end of the first day. Though it is a well-designed and well-developed course, they still felt frustrated. "What *they want* to do is to share their experiences with one another," he said. (These were auto dealers attending a seminar.) "If that's what they really want," I suggested, "start there. Begin with a session during which they are encouraged to share. Then let them know there will be time for more of that, either in the classroom or in the lounge." Don't keep the good stuff hidden until students have "learned the basics." It works like magic.

2. Move from the big picture into the details. Since you know the subject, *you* can think comfortably about any piece of it and understand where it fits into the whole. Students don't have that luxury. They don't know the territory; they need a map. That's what you're there for. So start with the biggest picture and then work toward the details.

    If equipment is involved, give your students an opportunity to get their hands on it before they do anything else and, if possible, teach them how to operate it before you teach them anything about how it works. The rule is this:

    > Don't expect students to think about the abstract until they have something concrete to think abstractly about.

    In other words, give them some experience with the "things" they're there to learn about—get the concepts into their muscles—before expecting them to be able to handle the abstract concepts relating to those things. For example, if you're teaching people how to repair engines or amplifiers, get them to see and feel and hear those things before you talk to them about nomenclature or how they work.

3. Give your students as many opportunities as possible to decide for themselves which module to work on at any given time. It will help keep them motivated. Naturally, the constraints imposed by the skill hierarchy and by your environment will dictate how many such options you can offer. The easiest way to let them know what the options are is by means of a course map. Such a map shows the entire course at a glance and shows which sequencing options are available at any given point in the course. Even if you don't have the freedom to provide sequencing options at the moment, you should know how to read and construct a course map.

Figure 17.1

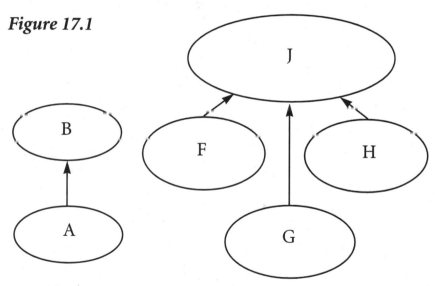

Master Module A before attempting Module B

Master Modules F, G, and H before attempting Module J. Modules F, G, and H may be mastered in any order.

Creating a Course Map

A course map is a simple graphic device through which to communicate some of the course procedures to your students. It shows each of the modules and the dependency relationship between them. For example, an arrow between two units tells students that they should first study the unit from which the arrow leads.

A course map also tells students that they should not study any module that has arrows leading into it before they have mastered *all* the units from which the arrows originate. And it tells them that modules shown in parallel may be studied in any order. Here's how to derive a course map from your hierarchy, your experience, and your knowledge of local constraints.

1. Get out your hierarchy and put the name of each module or skill on a quarter of a three-by-five card or scrap of paper (the little stickies—pads of paper with self-adhesive on one end—are ideal).

2. Push these bits and pieces around on a flipchart-size piece of paper until they depict the same relationships shown on your hierarchy. That's where you begin.

3. If two or three skills are closely related and will take very little time to learn, consider "collapsing" them into a single module.

4. Now think about the flow of the course. For example, if there are two skills that can be learned in any order, but your experience tells you that one of them should be attempted before the other, just move that module an inch or so toward the bottom of the paper. The two skills will still be shown as independent (there won't be a line between them), but the student will be guided to study the one closest to the bottom of the page before starting on the other.

If there are two or more independent objectives that should be accomplished before a third is attempted, draw arrows to show this dependency relationship. Students would then know that they can learn the two independent objectives in any order but that they would have to master both of them before attempting the third.

5. When you have all the items in a position that your experience and knowledge of the learning environment says will work, draw the map on the paper *in pencil.*

6. Explain your map to someone—anyone. Talk them through the map from bottom to top. Try to convince this person that you haven't imposed more sequencing restrictions than your subject matter and circumstances require. And then make the changes indicated.

Figure 17.2

Example #1: Here is a course map showing the sequence of modules to be completed by the students in our self-paced *Instructional Module Development Workshop* (Resource #16). Notice that though a couple of sequencing options are open to the student, the order of the lessons in this course is mostly prescribed. This is because students are expected to apply each skill learned to their own instructional project *in the order* in which these skills are used when developing a course.

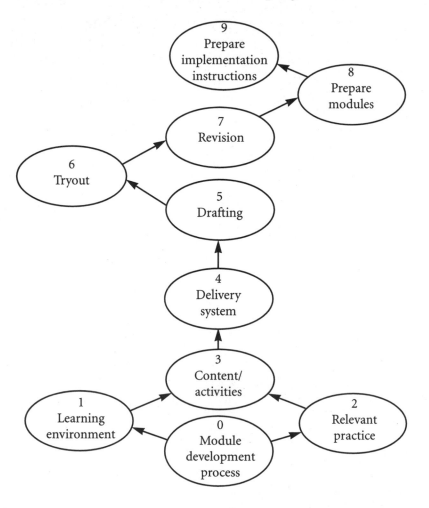

Example #2: Here is a portion of the course map used in the self-paced *Criterion-Referenced Instruction Workshop* (Resource #15). Notice that students have many options in sequencing their instruction. Though it is suggested (but not required) that they begin with modules closest to the bottom of the map, they are encouraged to work on whichever module is of interest at the time and for which they have satisfied the prerequisites.

Figure 17.3

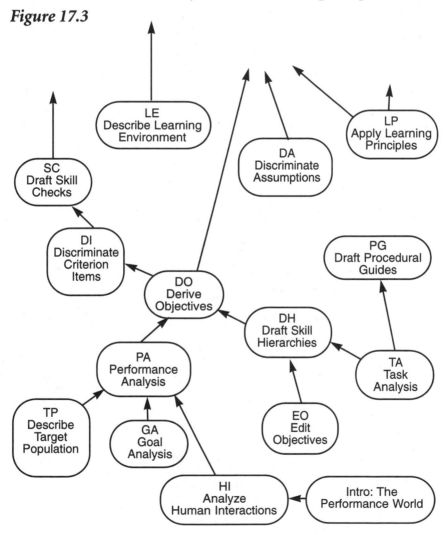

Example #3: This map is from a course called "Developing Performance Aids," created by Peter Pipe. Here the meaning of the horizontally dashed line is: The units below it are to be read, studied, and discussed; but because they are informational only (e.g., Module IN-2), there are no performance checks (criterion tests) associated with them.

The placement of modules DT-1 and ED-1 on the map expresses the best wisdom and experience of the author and says to the student, "While it is true that these modules have no prerequisites and may be studied at any time, you will find it more productive to study them sometime after you have completed module PA-1." Why then didn't the author draw a line between PA-1 and the other two modules? Because he didn't want to falsely suggest that PA-1 *must* be learned before DT-1 and ED-1 can be learned.

Figure 17.4

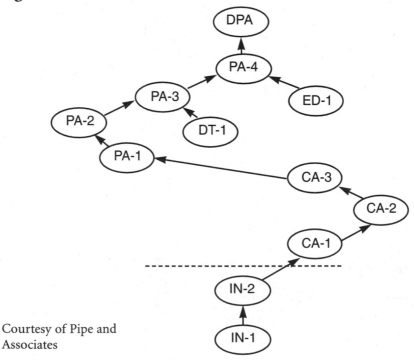

Courtesy of Pipe and
Associates

Example #4: Many years ago, when I taught introductory psychology at a university, all of us on the faculty knew what entering students were interested in. They were interested in sex, ESP, hypnosis, and the behavior of that weird roommate. But where did we begin the course? Why, with the history of psychology. We told them about the good old days when the crazies were chained in dungeons and about how . . . Zzzzzzzzzzzzzzzz. And then we'd sit around the faculty lounge, grousing about how students weren't motivated like they were when we went to school and scratching for things we could do to wake them up. What incredible naiveté—not to mention arrogance.

What should we have done? We should have started right on the first day with one of those topics of high interest. We wouldn't have had to do much with it, but it would have tugged the students further into the course by starting with something they were known to be interested in, and by promising more on that topic later on.

You don't arouse anyone's interest with the history of anything. Once you *have* aroused interest by helping them develop some skill and thereby some confidence, *then* students may become interested in the history. After all, learning about the history is one of the ways of "experiencing" a subject. But don't ever *begin* a course with history (unless it's a history course). Tell yourself that until students know something about your subject and have developed at least some feeling of competence, history is interesting only to you.

To Learn More: See Resources #8, #15, and #16.

Part V

Implementing the Instruction

18
Course Procedures

Situation: *You want to be sure to deliver your instruction while using procedures as close to the state of the art as your circumstances will allow.*

Suddenly the house lights dim, the orchestra plays a fanfare, and the instructor marches into the classroom bearing—Ta da!—examination papers.

Instr: Today we're going to have a mid-term exam!

You: (Shouting over the pandemonium) Wait a minute! You never said anything about a mid-term!

Instr: Come now. By now you should know that courses come equipped with exams.

You: But a mid-term? At the end of the first week? And without warning?

Instr: Oh, stop your whining. Now come up here and rap out a five-minute description of the theory of relativity.

That dialogue may seem a bit far-fetched, but I'll bet it isn't that far off from some of the experiences you've endured during your own academic career. But you wouldn't do that to *your* students, would you? Of course you wouldn't.

One of the ways to avoid this sort of dastardly deceit is to let students in on the secret of how you intend for the course to function—by giving them a copy of the course procedures up front.

What Are Course Procedures?

Course procedures are the rules by which courses are conducted. Though they may or may not be written down or recognized for what they are, every course operates by a set of rules or procedures. In one course the rule may be, "Tests will be given on the following dates _____," while in another the rule may be, "Take the test when you feel you have accomplished the objective of the module." The rule in still another course may be, "Add your name to the sign-up sheet, and you will be notified when the demonstration has been prepared." In still another course (the kind you've often experienced) the rule is, "I'm not going to *tell* you what the rules are. You'll just have to figure them out yourself." And so it goes. We have rules about when to arrive, when to leave, how to proceed, where to find things, how to get questions answered, and dozens of other things.

Whatever the procedures by which your course will be conducted, *they should be written down and in the hands of the students.* This will tell them what is expected of them and will eliminate their need to waste time "psyching out" the instructor. In addition, the very act of writing the course procedures will help you to derive the most efficient implementation strategy possible for the constraints under which you must function. Whatever you do, prepare a set of course procedures for your students and include them as the number-one item in every student's package of materials.

Where Do Course Procedures Come From?

But where do these procedures come from? How are they derived? After all, you wouldn't just sit down and dream up a set of rules at random. Neither would you write a set of rules that reflects the philosophy of "I'll teach *them* the same way that somebody taught me." That would be the amateur's way out and probably would result in instruction 40 years behind its time.

So how *do* we derive course procedures? We do it by developing rules that put ideal characteristics into practice as closely as local constraints will allow. This means that we compare an ideal or desired course characteristic with our own situation (space, equipment, budget, time, students) and then write one or more rules that will come as close as possible to implementing that ideal characteristic.

These ideal characteristics are derived from research, validated learning principles, and experience; they represent statements that describe what we would be doing if we developed and implemented our instruction in the very best way we know how. Here are some of the main ones.

Ideal Course Characteristics

1. *Instruction exists only where it is a solution or remedy for a problem in human performance.* If they already know how to do it, they don't need instruction. If they don't need to know how to do it, they don't need instruction.

2. *Instructional objectives have been derived from competent performance on the job.* This guarantees that there is a

need for the instruction and answers the question, "How much _____ should I teach?"

3. *Each student studies and practices only those skills not yet mastered to the level required by the objectives.* As a result, you won't waste time and student motivation by teaching them things they already know, but you'll give them enough practice to master the skills being taught.

4. *Student progress is controlled by their own competence.* Application of this characteristic prevents student time and motivation from being wasted by requiring more advanced students to wait while others catch up. It also means slower students won't have to short-change themselves on practice to keep up.

5. *Instruction is directly related to accomplishment of the objectives.* Most or all instruction time will be devoted to teaching what needs to be learned.

6. *Instructional materials impose a minimum of obstacles between the learners and the learning.* Thus, unnecessary impediments to learning are avoided.

7. *Instruction is presented through the simplest delivery systems consistent with the objectives, the learners, and the learning environment.* This saves time and money by ensuring that students will get the instruction they need through the simplest and most direct media that will do the job.

8. *Students are provided with an opportunity to practice each objective and to obtain task-diagnostic feedback regarding the quality of their performance.* (Note: Task-diagnostic feedback is explained in Chapter 20,

"Implementing the Instruction.") Learning is far more effective when students practice what they are learning, and when they receive properly formulated information (feedback) about how well they are doing.

9. *Learners receive repeated practice in skills that are used often or are difficult to learn.* Application of this characteristic ensures that difficult-to-learn and often-used skills will receive periodic refreshment during a course.

10. *Learners receive immediate feedback regarding the quality of their test performance.* This allows a test procedure also to be a learning experience, which is positive and useful. It will also avoid the problems caused by delayed feedback.

11. *Desired student performances are followed by consequences they consider favorable to them.* Because people learn to avoid punishing experiences, this practice will ensure that motivation is strengthened rather than weakened.

12. *Within the limits imposed by content, equipment constraints, and the course map, learners are free to sequence their own instruction.* That is, given the constraints just mentioned, at any given time students may select for study the topic in which they are most interested.

13. *The learning environment itself contains the facilities and equipment needed to implement the above characteristics.* This way neither you nor the student will waste time, become frustrated, or miss important things because of missing items or the need to retrieve items from remote locations (such as regional media centers).

14. *Students will learn to recognize correct and incorrect*

performance before being allowed to practice the skill being learned. This means that students will learn what is needed to make their practice sessions productive.

It is seldom possible to put all of these and other ideal characteristics into practice. There are, after all, time constraints, money constraints, and space and equipment constraints, to name a few. Therefore, course procedures are rules that will implement the ideal as closely as possible. In plain language, we try to derive course procedures that will allow us to say, "I am teaching absolutely as well as constraints will allow."

How to Do It

For each of the characteristics listed above, answer the following questions:

1. Can you implement the characteristic as stated?

2. If so, write a rule that will tell students what to do.

3. If not, say what prevents you from implementing the characteristic.

4. Can you think of a way to get around that constraint?

5. If so, take the action needed to get around the constraint, and then write the rule that will put the ideal characteristic into practice.

6. If not, can you think of a way to get around the constraint even a little bit? In other words, can you think of a way to reduce the obstacle that's preventing you from implementing the characteristic?

7. Take the action needed and then write a rule or rules that will come as close to implementing the characteristic as is possible.

Example: One of the ideal characteristics of instruction is "Student progress is controlled by their own competence." This means that the most efficient instruction is that which allows students to progress to something new as soon as they have mastered what they are learning now. It means that students are not forced to begin new material before they have mastered the old and that they are encouraged to progress to new material as soon as they have mastered the old.

> **NOTE:** Sometimes students will master a skill before developing the confidence needed to actually apply the skill. When this happens, they will often ask if they can practice a little more before moving on. If you can, let them practice. At other times you will find that students are so delighted with their new skill that they want to exercise it—fondle it—before moving on. When this happens, they are literally enjoying the subject matter; it feels good to do something you've just learned how to do. Unless time presses, it is good to allow this to happen.

To show you how to think through the questions above, I'll put some sample "thinking" in the form of a monologue. That way you can see what goes on in the head of someone deriving course procedures.

1. We are considering the characteristic "Student progress is controlled by their own competence." Can you implement the characteristic as stated?

   No way!

2. Write the rules.

   I can't do it.

3. What prevents you from implementing this characteristic?

   This school has always had a 50-minute hour, and instructors are expected to have all students progress at the same rate.

4. Can you think of a way to get around that constraint?

   Well, I suppose I could ask for a policy change, but it seems unlikely it would happen in my lifetime.

5. If so, take the action needed to get around the constraint.

   I can't think of a way around this constraint.

6. If not, can you think of a way to get around the constraint even a little bit?

   Well, I suppose I could make some changes within my own class period without even needing any change in policy. I could give the students the course objectives and the course materials and ask them to tell me when they are ready to demonstrate their skill. When they can perform OK, I could then let them go on to the next objective.

7. Take the action needed and then write the rule or rules that will come as close to implementing the characteristic as is possible.

   Course Procedures: *When you think you have accomplished an objective, you may ask for the test. If you can perform according to the standards (criteria), you may move ahead to the next objective.*

Let me offer a suggestion at this point. Whenever you find yourself saying, "I can't do it because it's against school policy," look a little closer. Many of these "policies" have never been written down, and many of them are fictional. They are only things that everyone believes. Question them.

Another thought. There are many things that you can do differently without ever having to ask for anyone's blessing or approval. After all, you're being paid to exercise your best judgment to get the job done. If you go to your administration or to your management for approval of every change you want to make, you'll soon earn a reputation for being unable to do anything on your own. So think about it. If you can change the color of the paper on which your tests are printed without requiring anyone else's approval, you can change the rules by which you operate your course. And if you can change some of your practices without demanding approval, you can come closer to implementing ideal instruction just by deciding to do it.

A Simpler Way

Here is a simpler way to derive course procedures. Use the model set of procedures listed below as your guide. It is a set of procedures used by those who are in a position to implement most or all ideal characteristics. Imagine that this will be the set of procedures by which you will implement your course. Where you see a procedure that you cannot implement, only then will you need to answer the questions above and make changes. The closer you can come to following these procedures, the closer you will be to applying what is known about making instruction work.

Model Course Procedures

Following are the procedures or rules by which this course is conducted. In general, the procedures tell you to select the module you want to study, to proceed at your own rate, to ask for the Skill Check when you are ready to do so, to work with others as much or as little as you wish, and to use as few or as many resources as you feel you need or want.

How to Begin

1. Read these Course Procedures.

2. Be sure you know the location of the resources, the Skill Checks, the Self-Evaluation material, and the Master Progress Plotter (the sheet that shows which modules you have completed).

3. Begin with Module _____. It is a short introductory unit that will show you the big picture and provide you with a mental map of where you are heading.

4. Use only the resources (readings, practice material) you feel you need to help you develop the skill defined by the objective of the module.

5. Practice the skill at least once before asking for the Skill Check.

6. Take time to muse, to talk to others, and to see how others are applying the skills they are learning. This is not a race. Use the opportunity to sharpen your skills.

Course Map

The Course Map shows how each module of the course is related to other modules and to the course as a whole.

1. Before beginning to study any module, complete all the prerequisites for that module (i.e., all modules shown by lines and arrows leading into that module).

2. The location of a module on the map represents a suggestion as to the approximate point in the course where it will be most meaningful to you. Where no sequence is shown (i.e., where there are no arrows leading into a module), feel free to study those modules in any order you wish.

3. Place an "X" or some other mark on those modules the instructor indicates are optional for you.

Modules

1. Before beginning a new module series, read the introductory comments at the front of the module material. The diagram facing the introduction shows how the modules in that section relate to the rest of the course.

2. Study only one module at a time, but feel free to put that module down and study another that you are eligible to enter whenever you wish.

3. Begin a module by reading the Objective and the description of the Skill Check (or sample test item).

4. When you feel qualified to do so, ask the instructor for the Skill Check. (It's a good idea, however, to read through the entire module so that there won't be any terminology surprises.)

5. Work through the module at your own speed.

6. If you are not sure of your competence, complete all the practice exercises. If you are still not sure, check with the instructor.

7. The instructor will provide a sign-up sheet for those modules that include group practice. Sign up for the session most convenient for you.

Resources

1. There are at least three sources of information for each module: the module itself, other students, and the instructor. Additional resources may also be available. If so, they are listed at the beginning of the module.

2. Consult any of the resources you think may help you, but do not feel compelled to consult them all.

3. When resources are listed in a module, the relevant page numbers are indicated. Feel free to read more widely if you wish, but keep the module objective in mind as you do.

4. Feel free to ask other students which resources they found most helpful; provide the same information for others if they ask.

5. Work with a colleague whenever you wish.

Skill Checks (Criterion Tests)

1. Ask for a Skill Check whenever you feel ready. Before doing so, however, you will save time if you first make sure you can answer "Yes" to these questions:

   a. Did I practice the skill called for by the objective?

   b. Did I get a colleague sign-off, if it is called for by the module?

2. If, after reviewing a module, you feel ready for the Skill Check without further study, go for it.

3. Take only one copy of the Skill Check. Feel free to write on the Skill Check.

4. If you do not perform adequately on a Skill Check, you will be asked, after further study or practice, to complete the same or similar Skill Check again, at the instructor's discretion.

5. When you have completed a Skill Check, check your work against the Self-Evaluation material. The instructor (or whomever else is qualified to do so) will then check your work.

Personal Progress Summary

1. Ask whomever is checking your work to date and initial your Personal Progress Summary next to the appropriate module. This is your verification that you have been checked off on that module and are free to move to another.

Master Progress Plotter

1. When your Personal Progress Summary has been initialed for a module, make sure the instructor makes the proper entry on the Master Progress Plotter. That will be your indication that your mastery has been recorded—and it will provide another reason to feel good about your progress.

End of Model Course Procedures

Optional Course Procedures

You may find a need to write other course procedures, depending on the nature and location of your course, the amount of equipment available, and the time available. Here are some examples:

- Complete all the modules below the line shown on the Course Map before working on those above it.

- When you have completed all the modules below the solid line shown on your Course Map, you will be eligible for the group practice session, minilecture, or demonstration. Sign up for it at that time.

- When a module asks you to complete a practice exercise, write directly on the worksheets supplied.

- Be sure to read the instructions before using the videotape recorder.

- You will find equipment to practice on in Room _____. This room will be open from 10 a.m.–noon, and from 3 p.m.-5 p.m.

- Before you enter the practice room, take one of the tags that is hanging on the door, and then replace it when you leave. Each tag represents an available practice station and will let other students know how many pieces of practice equipment are available at any given time.

- If the work you have completed for a Skill Check is not yet adequate, and if the instructor had to revise or modify it, it will be considered the instructor's work, and you will be asked to repeat the Skill Check after completing some additional practice.

- If, at any time during the course, you feel that there is too much reading, it is probably because you are doing one or more of the following:

    1. Working alone instead of with a colleague when a module suggests it.

    2. Plodding through a resource you consider uninteresting or inappropriate for you instead of putting it down and finding another.

    3. Using printed materials as your primary source of information instead of making use of colleagues and the course manager.

    4. Spending too long with a problem before asking for assistance.

    5. Working through *all* the resources listed in a module, instead of using only those you need to help you develop the desired skill.

To Learn More: See Resources #5, #8, #15, #16, and #17.

19
Getting Ready

Situation: *Your course has been prepared, and you know your subject. Before the course begins, however, you want to make sure that you know how to apply the key motivational techniques that will maximize student eagerness to learn.*

"Good morning. I'm your Geek instructor."

"Ever been to Geekland?"

"No."

"Know how to speak or read Geek?"

"Not yet."

"Know how to dress like a Geek?"

"Don't they wear plastic pen protectors?"

"Know anything about Geek culture?"

"Sorry. I've never met a Geek person."

"Goodbye!"

How's that for beating a dead horse—for trampling the obvious? Of course one needs to know the content of the instruction. How else would one know how to conduct demonstrations, provide clarifying explanations, and answer questions? How else would one gain credibility with the students? How can anyone teach something they don't know?

What may be a little less obvious is that there is more to making instruction work than just knowing the subject matter. Clearly, how you teach can be just as important as what you teach. So before entering the classroom, or computer, or video studio, you'll want to make sure that you can apply at least four of the important practices that have much to do with how well the instruction will work, and with how eager the students will be to learn more; success definitions, performance consequences, modeling, and self-efficacy.

Success Definitions

Recently I questioned several expert instructors individually about their vision of instructional success. I asked each of them, "What would things look like if your instruction were totally successful?" Though they used different words in their replies, the substance was quite similar. Here is a summary of how these instructors visualize instructional success.

1. Students leave the instruction having accomplished the objectives set out for them.

2. They are eager to apply what they learned.

3. They are eager to learn more.

4. They can speak coherently about what they have learned.

In other words, successful instruction sends students away who can do and are willing to do, who have a favorable attitude toward the subject and are eager to learn more. To make that happen you'll need to be especially attentive to what happens to your students *during* their learning. For example, students who are rewarded for arriving late (by having already-covered material explained to them) have no incentive to learn to be prompt. And if you value promptness you will have lost an opportunity to make it blossom.

So how can you arrange things so that students will be most likely to leave with the characteristics you deem valuable? By *learning how to identify desired student performances,* so that you can smile on them when they appear and take corrective action when they don't. Take a few minutes to make a list of the things you consider to be productive (desired) student performances. Answer the question, "What things do I want my students to do while learning, and as a result of learning?" Here is a start on your list of desired student behaviors:

- Arrive prepared to work.

- Ask questions when something is not clear.

- Ask for additional practice material.

- Be willing to practice until the objective has been mastered.

- Offer to help other students.

- Keep trying until they can perform as desired.

- Be willing to spend time maintaining tools and equipment.

- Be anxious to demonstrate their competence and apply their new skills.

- Make favorable comments about the subject they are learning.

(Add your items here)

How does a success definition promote effective instruction? Once you have a clear picture in your mind that tells you how to recognize instances of desired outcomes (evidence of success), and of approximations to desired outcomes, you'll be able to follow those desired outcomes with favorable consequences (to the student). That will make it more, rather than less, likely that you'll get more of those desired outcomes. (As you know, a new skill often looks somewhat shaky—less than wonderful. If you don't recognize it as an acceptable approximation along the road to mastery, you might kill it off.)

Consequences

With a picture of instructional success clearly in mind, you can think about what you will do when the successes (and the approximations toward success) actually occur.

Because instructor behavior is so critical to successful instruction, you must pay careful attention to how you behave in the presence of your students. Whether you like it or not, you are an instrument of reward and punishment, an instrument that will cause students either to want to learn more of your subject or to want to hear no more about it. Whether you like it or not, your own behavior shapes the attitudes of your students. For example, consider the effects of the following instructor statements:

> "Look. This is a dumb video, but I'm supposed to show it, and you're supposed to watch it."

> "I already answered that question three weeks ago."

> "If that's the best you can do, maybe you should be in some other department."

> "Don't try to get ahead of the class."

> "This class isn't as sharp as the one I had *last* year."

"Fifty percent of this class won't be here a month from now."

"I grade on a curve, so no matter how competent you are, some of you will have to get low grades."

"I'm not the one who designed this course."

If you think back over your own academic history, you'll think of dozens of examples of instructor behavior that served only to turn students off. The sad thing is that these events occurred mostly because the instructors were unaware of the effects of what they were doing. Fortunately, there is a way to avoid the accidental turn-offs and to maximize the deliberate turn-ons. Here's how.

Learn to identify the favorable consequences under your control. For example, you can smile or not smile. If you smile on undesired performance, either accidentally or because you don't know any better, you may get more of it. If you offer the equivalent of a pat on the back when a student is goofing off, you may get more of that, too.

If, on the other hand, you frown or somehow insult or demean a student for asking questions or for trying, you'll get less of those positive efforts. So make a list of the things you might do in response to desired performance. And if you're thinking, "There's nothing I can do," you've never been more wrong. You ought to be able to list at least two dozen things that you could do to encourage desired performance when you see it, none of which have anything to do with money. I'll help you get your list started:

- a smile

- a favorable comment

- a little extra attention

- a little time off (even a few minutes works)

- ask the student to explain a concept to others

- applause

Add your own.

-

-

-

Check your own performance. The easiest and most private way to find out whether you are encouraging desired performance and discouraging undesired performance is to set up a video camera in the back of the classroom or lab and just let it record.

Review the tape in private. Look for examples of desired student performance, and then watch to see what you did in response—when the desired performance happened. Did you ignore it? Did you punish it? Or did you pay attention to it, smile on it, say something nice about it? Build on it? This simple review will show you how you might modify your own performance so that you will get more of what you want and less of what you don't want. Your goal should be to "glow" on desired (productive) performances, and to ignore unproductive performances wherever possible.

People See, People Do

Instructional success is also influenced by the quality of the modeling—by what they see and hear the instructor do while they're in the instructor's presence.

Instructors who tell students to do something one way and then do it (model) another will find their students becoming inattentive to their words. Instructors who demonstrate apathy or indifference to what they are teaching will soon find their students doing the same. Instructors who model enthusiasm for their subject and for learning, however, will often find these characteristics rubbing off onto their students.

Few truths have been as well established by research as the fact that most of what we learn during our lives is learned by imitation. We see things done and we try to do likewise. We read about how things are done, our instructors show and tell how they are done, and we try to do likewise. To paraphrase Dr. Albert Bandura, if we learned mainly by trial and error, world population would be a lot smaller than it is; a lot fewer of us would survive adolescence.

Because modeling is such a powerful instructor, it is imperative to instructional success that you do as you want others to do, that you act as you want your students to act, lest you accidentally reduce their interest in the subject you are teaching. Here is a summary of the main modeling principles and an example to illustrate how each might be applied:

1. Observers learn by watching and imitating others; they tend to behave as they have seen others behave.

   Application example: If you want students to follow certain safety precautions, then you follow them—especially when you are in their presence.

2. Observers will be more likely to imitate a model who has prestige in the observers' eyes.

   Application example: Have desired performance demonstrated by someone your students respect: a manager, local hero, football player, rock star. If you have prestige in the eyes of your students, it is doubly important for you to practice what you preach.

3. Observers will be more likely to imitate modeled performance when they see the model being rewarded for that performance.

   Application example: When one student performs to expectations, make sure you respond positively to that performance (e.g., with a smile, favorable comment, token). Other students will be more likely to imitate the desired performance.

4. Observers who see a model being punished will be less likely to imitate the performance that was punished.

   Application example: If a student is punished (demeaned, insulted, ridiculed) for attempting a difficult task and making a mistake, other students will be less likely to attempt the difficult task themselves.

Unhappily, you may not be able to tell when you are accidentally putting students down. (I recall an excellent instructor who took all students' questions seriously. But while he thought about an answer, he would scowl and tug at an eyebrow, which intimidated the other students and made them reluctant to ask their own questions.) Fortunately, there is a simple solution. As previously suggested, put a video camera in the back of your classroom and let it record as you teach. At your convenience you can review the tape while pretending to be a student. You will easily be able to spot the opportunities for improvement.

Self-Efficacy

Instruction that works not only sends students away with the ability to do what the course objectives require, but it also sends them away with the eagerness to apply what they have learned and with the perseverance needed to overcome obstacles. In other words, successful instruction sends students away with high, rather than low, self-efficacy. You influence the strength of your students' self-efficacy whether you like it or not.

What is Self-Efficacy?

Self-efficacy refers to people's judgments about their capability to execute specific courses of action; it refers to their belief in their ability to perform specific tasks or apply specific skills. Self-efficacy isn't concerned with *actual* skills and abilities, but with people's *beliefs* about the strength of those skills and abilities.

People who say with confidence, "I can climb an elephant blindfolded," and then proceed to do so, have high self-efficacy toward elephant-climbing. Because of their strong self-efficacy, they will be more willing to climb elephants in the future, and they will be more likely to brush themselves off and try again when they fall off. Those who are equally skilled at elephant-climbing (or anything else), but who judge themselves to be poor at this critical skill will be less likely to be willing to practice the skill, and will be less likely to persevere in the face of setbacks. You can see the importance of having strong self-efficacy toward the things you can do well.

Self-efficacy is not necessarily related to level of skill, because people may or may not make accurate judgments about the strength of their abilities. Everyone knows someone who is better at something than they judge themselves to be. "Aw, shucks," they may say, "I'm not really very good at that," even though they may in fact be the best in the business.

Because such people are handicapped in their ability to succeed, and because instructors and parents are the most common causes of low self-efficacy, the importance of learning how to strengthen self-efficacy in your students cannot be overstated.

How is Self-Efficacy Strengthened?

The goal is to facilitate a match between an actual level of skill and self-judgments about that level of skill, so that people really believe they can do what they can in fact do. Here's how.

1. **Performance mastery.** The most powerful action is to make sure your students are given an opportunity to practice until they achieve mastery, and to help them to perceive that they have, in fact, mastered. Help them to understand that their mastery came about as the result of their own efforts, rather than as a result of the instructor's efforts, or because of a job aid, or because of luck.

2. **Feedback.** Provide task-diagnostic, rather than self-diagnostic, feedback for practice efforts.

   Self-diagnostic feedback interprets less-than-perfect performance as a personal deficiency. "You just aren't motivated enough;" "Maybe you just don't have the talent for this work;" "How many times will I have to tell you this?" "You're just not good at this." "You're not working up to your potential." Self-diagnostic feedback blames imperfect performance on failings of the individual.

   Task-diagnostic feedback focuses on the task being performed. Failure is used as information through which the performance may be improved, rather than as evidence of incompetence. "If you'll put your hand in this position rather than that one, I think you'll see some improvement;" "If you stand in front of the elephant rather than behind it, you'll have more things to hold onto as you climb;" "If you'll hold a drinking straw between your lips, you'll actually be able to see the improvement in your lip control as you practice." Task-diagnostic feedback focuses on ways in which performance of a task may be improved.

3. **Modeling.** Self-efficacy can be improved when students watch others like themselves performing competently. (Refer to the modeling discussion in the previous section.)

4. **Social persuasion.** Self-efficacy is influenced by the comments of others (we all know the powerful effects that unkind comments can have). Arrange for success experiences and then help students interpret those success experiences as indications of improvement. Your own comments and actions are always influencing the self-efficacy of your students, either favorably or unfavorably. You cannot choose to use or not use social persuasion, so you must be careful about your behavior when in the presence of your students. Keep it positive.

5. **Physiological information.** Sometimes people will make judgments about their ability, or lack of it, from physiological cues: aches, pains, effort, etc. They will confuse the difficulty of a task with their ability to perform it. "Gee, I'm not very good at this—this is hard." Lots of things are difficult to do, but lots of people become very good at doing them. Help your students to understand the difference between hard work and skill

level. Make sure they understand that the need to work hard at something shouldn't be misinterpreted as a lack of skill.

To Learn More: See Resources #4, #12, #13, #15, #17, #19, and #20.

20

Implementing the Instruction

Situation: Everything has been prepared, you're pre-pared, and students are about to arrive.

Now you're ready to begin the instruction. You may do it primarily through lecture, through a self-paced format, through a "distance learning" format, through computer or video, or through some combination of these formats. These delivery formats tend to clump themselves into two basic variations:

1. *Instructor-controlled,* where the instructor controls the flow of events (e.g., lectures in the classroom, lectures by video), and

2. *Performance-controlled,* where learning activities are controlled by student progress toward accomplishment of an objective (e.g., usually through self-paced formats).

Instructor-Controlled Instruction

In this traditional format the instructor is the primary source of information, usually offered to students in the form of presentations (lectures). The main advantage is that a single instructor can present information to as many students as can be brought within eye- and earshot, which, through the use of television and satellites, can amount to millions.

The main disadvantages are that instructors need to be taught, though often they are not, how to be good presenters; individual attention is difficult (and in some cases, even impossible) to maintain; all students must receive the same instruction in the same way and at the same pace; and students cannot practice individually for as long as they need to become proficient in each of the objectives.

Performance-Controlled Instruction

In this format students' progress is controlled by their own performance. Students exert some control over their learning activities, in that when they have mastered one objective, they are encouraged to move to the next. This is a highly flexible format that can accommodate instructor-led presentations as well as group sessions when they are called for by the objectives. Performance-controlled instruction is usually conducted in a self-paced mode.

The advantages of this format are that (a) each student has the opportunity to study and practice until all objectives are accomplished, (b) students often have some control over the sequence in which they address the modules, (c) instructors can devote most of their time to coaching individual students, and (d) all principles of learning can be applied toward effective performance. Another advantage is that the instruction can be guaranteed to accomplish the objectives that analysis has revealed to be important.

Disadvantages are that (a) instructors require some coaching before they can manage this format, and (b) some instructors find it difficult or impossible to handle this type of performance-oriented structure (they would rather perform than coach). Another "disadvantage" is that lead time is required to prepare the materials. Though this is also true of the instructor-led format, instructors have so often been expected to "wing it" (instruct without preparation) that many people erroneously believe that good instructor-led instruction takes little or no preparation, while a performance-based course takes more preparation time than is reasonable.

Here's how instruction is managed in both instructor-controlled and performance-controlled formats.

Managing Instructor-Controlled Instruction

No matter what the format of your instruction, you will always have occasion to present information by means of the lecture. When this is the case, you are acting as a transmitter, a broadcaster, of information, and your own behavior, as always, is critical. For example, if students cannot easily understand your words, all your preparation and all your expertise will be of little value. If your diction is poor, or your accent difficult to understand, you yourself become an obstacle to learning.

There are other characteristics that a good presenter (lecturer) should have if he or she is to facilitate learning rather than interfere with it. Here is a list. The effective presenter:

1. speaks clearly and understandably,

2. has mastery of the subject matter,

3. models desired student performance,

4. models enthusiasm for the subject and for learning,

5. provides positive consequences for desired performance,

6. can operate instructional equipment,

7. uses visuals in a timely manner and without causing distraction,

8. diagnoses individual student problems and recommends remedies, and

9. can handle a variety of instructional methods (e.g., discussions, question-and-answer sessions, role-plays).

Whether you are experienced or inexperienced, your presentations will benefit from periodic checkups. Because we are prone to picking up distracting mannerisms...er...ah...and gestures over time, the wise instructor periodically reviews his or her presentation behavior at least twice a year. This is done by using one or both of the following procedures:

1. Videotape one of your presentations, and then pretend you're a student and review it in private as you answer the checklist questions found in the "How to Do It" section below, and/or

2. Give your students a copy of the Presentation Checklist and ask each of them to complete it at the end of one of your presentations.

Since the instructor is the key instrument through which instruction is offered in the instructor-controlled format, it is important that that instrument (the instructor) be kept in fine tune.

How to Do It

Though just about everyone can talk, not everyone can deliver a presentation in a way that will teach. To make the presentation accomplish its purpose it needs to have certain characteristics. Here are the basic steps.

1. Before you begin, make sure you and your students have all the material needed for the lesson at hand.

2. Make sure the students are as comfortable as you can make them (temperature, adequate lighting, etc.), and make sure they can see everything that you will be doing.

3. Explain the objective of the lesson—students should have a written copy of their own to refer to. If this isn't the first lecture in the series, spend a minute or two reviewing what came before. (If you are using a course map, refer to it to remind students of the bigger picture.)

4. Explain/demonstrate why what they are about to learn is important to *them*.

5. Follow your lesson plan (described in Chapter 15).

6. Allow students to spend as much lesson time as possible practicing.

7. Then find out how well each student can perform the objective being learned. (This is much more difficult to do in the instructor-led format than the performance-controlled format, but do your best.)

Here is a Presentation Checklist to help remind you of the key features of a successful presentation. This Checklist is worded to be completed by the student. Marks in any but the Yes column represent opportunities for improvement.

Presentation Checklist	Yes	No	?
1. Was the objective of the session clear to you?			
2. Was it clear *why* the content or skill is important to *you?*			
3. Did the body of the presentation seem organized from your point of view?			
4. Were you "taught" only the things you didn't already know?			
5. Did you have opportunities to ask questions?			
6. Did you get helpful answers to those questions?			
7. Did you have an opportunity to practice what you were taught?			
8. Was your practice followed by prompt and useful feedback?			
9. Was the instructor easy to understand?			
10. Did the instructor seem interested in what was being taught?			
11. Did the instructor avoid doing anything to belittle, insult, or demean you or other students?			
12. Did the instructor avoid distracting mannerisms?			
13. Did you accomplish the objective of the lesson (module)? That is, can you now perform as the objective describes?			

Managing Performance-Controlled Instruction

In this format the instructor functions more as a coach than as a performer. Though the instructor is encouraged to instruct where necessary, the main burden of the instruction is carried by other media, such as audiotapes, videos, CDs, print (manuals, tests, booklets), simulators, or computers. Nonetheless, the instructor provides critical functions: makes resources available when needed, diagnoses student problems, instructs when necessary, and verifies performance progress. Though the course may be self-paced, it is not conducted without an instructor (unless it is designed to be a self-study course). In fact, this format recognizes that instructor time is too valuable to be wasted on matters that can be better handled through other means.

Instructors using this format have a great deal more control over learning progress than those using the instructor-led mode. When students have to demonstrate an ability to perform on one objective before they are encouraged to move to another, the instructor can have constant and instant knowledge of where each student is in relation to course completion and can take immediate remedial actions when needed.

If you have occasion to conduct a performance-controlled course, you will need to think of yourself as a coach or consultant rather than as the main dispenser of information. You will spend most of your time assisting individual students: diagnosing their difficulties and recommending corrective action, providing additional practice opportunities, reviewing performance and offering feedback, and reinforcing (glowing on) student successes and partial successes.

In addition to the skills listed earlier for classroom presenters, you will need only to develop your coaching skill to the point where you can sit with an individual student and calmly provide answers to questions, demonstrate a procedure, let the student make "safe" mistakes, and review performance. Because you will be physically closer to the student than when you are standing in front of a classroom, you will need to modify your gestures; sweeping gestures are fine when you are lecturing but inappropriate when working with individuals. You don't want to run the risk of knocking their glasses off or giving them a bloody nose while you're explaining a concept.

For the same reason, you will want to make sure you don't create other obstacles to learning as would be the case, for example, if you had bad breath. (We can't use course managers in our own workshops who are smokers, for example, even though they don't smoke in the classroom; that's because almost all of our participant non-smokers try to avoid sitting close to those who smell of stale tobacco.)

How to Do It

When you are ready to conduct a performance-controlled course in a self-paced manner, here are the steps to follow.

1. Begin with an orientation session. Explain to students what the course will be about, and hand out a copy of the objectives. Answer questions so that everyone knows what they will be expected to be able to do to be considered competent.

2. Hand out a copy of the course procedures and make sure everyone understands the rules by which you will be operating. They won't believe you at first no matter what you tell them, so you will have to repeat this information from time to time, and you will have to be sure to follow the procedures yourself.

3. Make sure students know where to locate all the resources, and explain the items uppermost in their minds at this time (i.e., what the hours are, where the bathroom is, and information about lunch).

4. Tell them how to begin the course. Make sure they each have a copy of the course map, and explain the options and constraints. Make sure everyone understands any symbols or conventions you have used in drawing the map, and make sure they understand what to do as soon as you end the orientation session.

5. As soon as the orientation session is over, wander around from student to student and remind them again where and how to begin. This may be the first time they have been given an opportunity to have anything to say about their own learning, so give them time to adjust. It may take up to a day or two to get into the flow of things, after which there will be no stopping them.

6. Follow the course procedures.

7. When a participant has accomplished all the objectives, provide a certificate of achievement (which actually means they have achieved, not just that they showed up), and ask the participant to complete a short question-naire intended to identify opportunities for course improvement.

To Learn More: See Resources #13, #15, #17, and #19.

Part VI

Improving the Instruction

21

Course Improvement

Situation: You want to locate opportunities for improving your existing instruction and to discover which changes will give the most benefit for the least effort.

A course is *effective* to the degree that it accomplishes what it sets out to accomplish. It is *efficient* to the degree it accomplishes its purpose with the least motion (time, effort, money). Since nothing is perfect, everything can be improved, including instruction. But just because instruction *can* be improved is not enough reason to go to expensive lengths to do so. If the instruction is doing what it is supposed to do, if it is doing so without undue cost, and if it is sending students away with more rather than less interest in the subject, it should be considered successful. Although you should make improvements when the need or opportunity arises, and you should make efforts to detect opportunities for improvement, a constant (and usually expensive) hunt for *perfection* is not a cost-effective use of your time.

Having said that, let's consider course improvement. This is something you do all the time. You do it when you refine your lesson plans, you do it when you make equipment more readily available to your students, you do it when you make the objectives a little easier to understand, and you do it when you make the instruction more tightly related to the objectives.

Improvement Requires Change

Though it is always necessary to change something in order to improve it, change doesn't always lead to improvement, Madison Avenue and politicians notwithstanding! To improve something means to make one or more of its characteristics come closer to some ideal or desired state. But you can claim that improvements have been made only if you know what you are trying to achieve, if you know the objectives you are trying to accomplish. For example, if you can say, "Hey, there; I gave a thirty-minute talk today and only said 'aah . . .' twelve times compared to yesterday's 'leventy-seven times," *and* if aah-less speech is the goal, standard, or ideal you are trying to achieve, *then* you can say that you have made an improvement.

Think of it this way. Improvement is the last of a four-step process.

1. **Measurement.** The first step is measurement. When you determine the extent of some characteristic, you are measuring. For example, "It's six feet long" is a statement about a measurement.

2. **Evaluation.** When you make a judgment based on a comparison of a measurement with a standard, you are evaluating. For example, "It's too short" is a statement of judgment. The thing measured has been compared against a standard or ideal and found not to match. Without a standard against which to compare a measurement, you cannot tell whether the thing measured is OK or not OK.

3. **Opportunities for improvement.** When your evaluations reveal discrepancies between measurements and standards, you identify opportunities for improvement. For example, "Five percent of my students didn't accomplish *all* their objectives during the time allotted, but they all should have," means that there was a discrepancy between the percent completing and the *desired* percent completing. It also means that an opportunity for improvement has been identified.

4. **Improvement.** Improvement is the result of action taken to cause one or more characteristics to move closer to the ideal or desired condition. For example, "I increased the amount of practice time, and now only one percent of my students don't accomplish all the objectives in the time available" means that action has been taken to successfully reduce the difference between what exists and what is desired.

What Should I Measure?

Depends on what you want to know. With all the statistical techniques that are available, it would be possible to collect mountains of numbers about a course. But most of them would be worthless. Why? Simply because most of that information would be of no use in making practical improvements. Most of it would simply amount to counting angels dancing on the head of a pin (which is a waste of time since we already know the answer is 42). So relax. Course improvement is relatively easy if you keep your eye on the possible.

As I said, what you measure is determined by what you want to know. So what *do* you want to know about your course? As soon as you decide what you want to know, you will know what to measure. There are three main things you should want to know about your course.

1. **Does it work?** Is it effective? Does it do what it's supposed to do?

2. **Is it of value?** Does it fill a need, either of the student or of the institution or organization?

3. **Is it efficient?** Is it up to date? Does it match the state of the art? Does it impose minimum obstacles between the student and the learning?

When to Do It

The first question (Does it work?) should be answered as each lesson or module is completed, and again (if appropriate) at the end of the course.

The second question (Is it of value?) should be answered during the analysis phase, i.e., before instruction is developed, and then periodically after the course has been put on line.

The third question (Is it efficient?) should be answered continually throughout the course, and at the end of the course when you scan the reaction sheets for opportunities for improvement.

How to Do It

Figure 21.1 will help you to visualize the method for answering the three key questions. Read the graphic clockwise like this: We start in the "real world"—from a real need, whether that be to teach someone to perform a job, to be prepared for the next course(s), or to function more successfully in some type of community. Then, through the analysis procedures, we derive the objectives of the instruction. We then develop instruction intended to accomplish those objectives. Through the instruction we develop competent students and then send them off to that portion of the world for which we have prepared them.

Figure 21.1

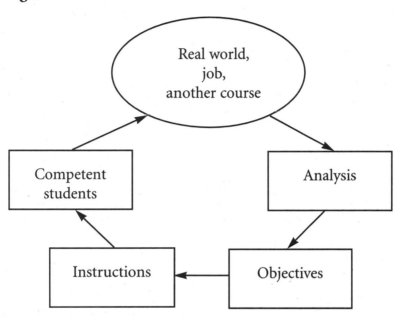

Here's how to think about answering the three key questions:

1. **Does it work?** This question is answered by comparing student performance with the objectives of the instruction (See Figure 21.2). It is *not* answered by looking at the content of the instruction, at the instructional procedures, or at what people are doing on the job. (By now you know that there are several factors that influence what people actually do on a job, or in a classroom, and that skill is only one of them. In other words, there are many reasons why people may not do what they know how to do. That's why it is not possible to assess whether

training works by watching their "real-world" performance.)

For example, if 95 percent of the students accomplished the objectives, then the course is "working" for 95 percent of the students. If 100 percent is the desired number, then there is an opportunity for improvement.

Figure 21.2

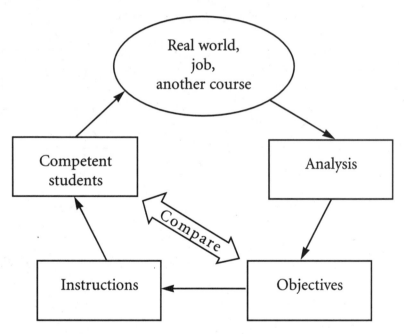

2. **Is it of value?** This question is answered by comparing the objectives of the instruction with the needs that gave rise to them (see Figure 21.3). In other words, this question is answered by verifying the accuracy of the analysis that led to the objectives, by comparing the objectives with the need. It is not answered by looking at the content of the instruction or at the instructional procedures.

If students no longer need to be able to do some of the things taught in the course or need to learn things not currently taught, then the opportunity for improvement lies in adjusting the objectives to meet the current need.

Thus the question, "Does it work?" is answered by determining whether the instruction does what it *sets out to do,* and the question, "Is it of value?" is answered by determining whether the instruction sets out to do something that *needs doing.*

Figure 21.3

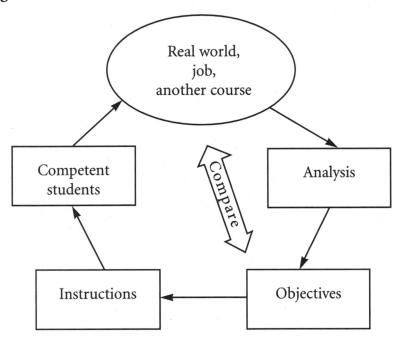

3. **Is it efficient?** This question is answered by comparing the instructional practices against the state of the art (expressed in terms of ideal characteristics), that is, by determining how closely those practices match the ideal

characteristics (see Figure 21.4). For example, if you noted that your tests did not yet match your objectives (for whatever reason), then you would have noted a discrepancy between what you *had* and what you *could* have had if your tests matched the state of the art, and you would have identified an opportunity for improvement. For another example, if you noted that students were not allowed to progress on the basis of their competence, you would have noted a discrepancy between what you were doing and what you should do, and identified another opportunity for improvement.

Figure 21.4

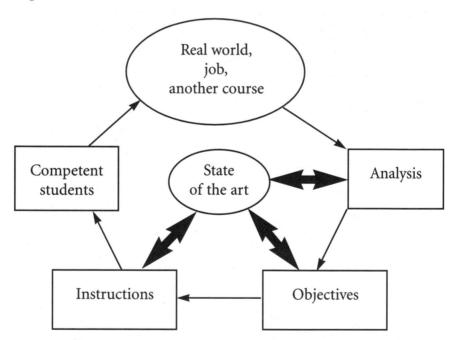

Here is a checklist of some questions that will help you spot opportunities for improvement. (The checklist also works as an excellent tool for auditing or assessing the effectiveness of training courses implemented as part of a quality management system.) You can derive your own list by reviewing the ideal characteristics presented in Chapter 18 and preparing questions that will allow you to determine just how well the course currently implements each of them.

Course Improvement Checklist

A check-mark in any but the "Yes" column represents an improvement opportunity.

Objectives

	Yes	No	?
1. Do you have objectives for your course, stated in performance terms?			
2. Are the objectives derived from the job, craft, or vocation being taught?			
3. If your students feed into another course, are your objectives derived in part from the prerequisites of that course?			
4. Were the objectives derived from some part of the real world (i.e., derived to meet a real need)?			

Course Materials

	Yes	No	?
1. Does each student have a copy of the course objectives?			
2. Is the instructional content confined to what is needed to accomplish the objectives (i.e., includes no irrelevant instruction)?			
3. Are the instructional materials all keyed to the objectives so that students know which materials are relevant to the accomplishment of each objective?			
4. Are the materials understandable to the students? (Ask them.)			
5. Are the instructional materials readily available to students in the learning environment?			

Learning Environment	Yes	No	?
1. Does each student have a copy of the course procedures (the rules by which the course is conducted)?			
2. Do students report that these procedures are actually followed?			
3. Do students have a course map or similar document showing how all the skills of the course relate to one another?			
4. Do course procedures pose a minimum of obstacles between students and the learning (i.e., do course procedures facilitate rather than hinder learning)?			
5. Are trainees free to move around the learning environment (subject to safety restrictions and group-related restrictions dictated by course objectives)?			
6. Do students have immediate access to course components such as texts, manuals, equipment, parts, diagrams, videotapes?			
7. Is the environment free of avoidable distractions such as noise, interruptions, discomfort, harsh or low lighting, uncomfortable temperature?			

Practice

	Yes	No	?
1. Does each learner practice each key skill?			
2. Is immediate feedback provided for practice exercises?			
3. Can each student practice until the objective has been accomplished?			
4. Is at least half the instruction time devoted to practice?			

	Yes	No	?
Instructor			
1. Has the instructor had training in:			
a. Classroom presentation skills? If not, have steps been taken to assure that the presentations match the characteristics of the Presentation Checklist on page 244?			
b. Instructional development? If not, will he/she promise to make the improvements suggested by this checklist?			
2. Does the instructor model the performance expected of the students? (Ask the students.)			
3. Does the instructor behave positively toward students rather than belittle or insult them? (Ask the students.)			
4. Does the instructor behave positively toward the subject he/she is teaching; i.e., model enthusiasm? (Ask the students.)			
5. Does the instructor show pride in the students' growing competence? (Ask the students.)			
6. Does the instructor make himself/herself available to assist individual students during the learning session?			

Students

	Yes	No	?
1. Do students exhibit a strong desire to learn what is being taught?			
2. Are students encouraged to practice only those skills in which they need improvement?			
3. Are students allowed some choice in the sequencing of their study?			
4. Are students allowed some choice in the method of learning and in the instructional resources they use?			
5. Are students allowed to practice until they have accomplished an objective?			
6. Do students receive individual attention when they need it?			
7. Are students encouraged to move to another unit of instruction when their competence has been demonstrated on the present one?			
8. Does something desirable happen to the students (from their point of view) when they reach competence in all the objcctives (e.g., favorable comments, cheers, applause, diploma, time off)?			

Performance Tests (Skill Checks)	Yes	No	?
1. Are students encouraged to demonstrate their competence (complete the skill check for the unit they are studying) when they feel ready to do so?			
2. Does every test item measure a course skill (i.e., does each item match the objective it is measuring in terms of performance and conditions)?			
3. Do students receive immediate and constructive feedback on their test performance?			
4. When a student's performance is judged to be not yet competent, is the weakness diagnosed and additional assistance given—without belittling the student?			
5. Is the student required to demonstrate competence in each key skill before being considered competent in the skills being taught?			

Opportunities Knocking

Once you've spotted improvement opportunities, you'll want some guidelines for sorting them out. It's one thing to spot an opportunity for improvement; it's something else to decide whether the improvement is worth making. Sometimes an improvement would cost far more than it is worth. For example, suppose you find a way to shorten a course by 10 percent. That would be worth thinking about doing, especially if the shorter course would be just as effective. But suppose the cost of that potential improvement would be far greater than the value of the improvement?

For another example, suppose you note that you could make the course work a lot better (improve the effectiveness) by letting students work for 4-hour stretches over 5 consecutive days, rather than for 50 minutes 3 times each week for **X** weeks. And suppose you also know that you'd have about as much chance of changing local policy as a goose has of running a marathon on a pogo stick. What to do? Look for other opportunities. Here's a way to think about the priority for taking advantage of the opportunities.

Attack Rules

1. *Fast fixes.* Make the easiest changes first, regardless of the payoff. For example, if you spot a dozen opportunities for improvement, and the easiest to implement would be to make your overheads more readable, do that first, even though it may add only a little to the effectiveness of your instruction. Making the easiest fixes first will get you moving and will give you some fast successes about which to feel good.

2. *Independent fixes.* Make the changes that don't require

the assistance or approval of someone else, regardless of payoff. If you can improve the course a little bit today, that's at least as good as improving it a lot next year. For example, if you could make your tests match your objectives without needing approval to do so, that would be a higher priority change than that of trying to get approval to teach your course in a single 40-hour block.

3. **High payoff fixes.** Make the fixes that will provide the highest payoff in course effectiveness, even if approval is required. Here is the list of actions that will give you the most return for your efforts, in order of priority:

   a. *Make objectives match the need.* Check your objectives against the need from which they were derived to make sure that they describe what students need to be able to do.

   b. *Provide outcome information to students.* If you do nothing else, make sure that a copy of the objectives is in the hands of the students. This act will give them a fighting chance of accomplishing what they need to accomplish, even though instructional materials may be scarce or poorly crafted.

   c. *Provide a reason to learn.* Once students know what is expected of them, the next best thing to do is to make sure they have a solid reason to learn. So make those changes that will help students perceive how it is important to them to accomplish the objectives, and remember that "Someday this will be important to you" is not a reason to learn. Instead, it is merely a symptom of instruction that hasn't yet been made relevant to the students.

d. *Provide as much practice time as possible.* Arrange the instruction so that students can practice when they are ready, for as long as they need to achieve mastery of the objective. Make sure they find out how well they are progressing.

e. *Provide instructional resources.* Give students whatever materials and other resources are currently available, regardless of their quality. When students want to learn, they'll do it in spite of inadequate resources.

4. **Supportive environment.** Once the above steps have been attended to, the best way to improve the quality and efficiency of your instruction is to improve the learning environment itself.

- Provide easy access to resources. Make sure that as many resources are available in the classroom itself as possible and that access isn't restricted by unnecessary bureaucratic rules.

- Minimize obstacles such as distractions, whether these are provided by noise, students, instructors, or outsiders.

- Make sure students know it's OK to practice and perform as desired and that it's OK to make mistakes while learning.

- Be available to help, but stay out of their way.

- Offer positive consequences for desired performance, as well as for performances that *approximate* the final desired performance.

- Make your feedback comments task-diagnostic, and gently correct your students when they make self-diagnostic comments.

5. *Adopt more streamlined procedures.* Go back to your course procedures and see where you can modify them to more closely approximate the ideal instructional characteristics found in Chapter 18.

6. *Improve the instruction itself.* Polish the presentations, hone the examples, and clarify the demonstrations. It may come as a surprise that this item is on the bottom of the priority list. But think about it a moment. What good is it to improve the elegance of the instruction itself if that instruction serves no useful purpose, or if everyone is convinced that it is of little or no value to them, or if students can already perform as desired? How much will it add to the effectiveness or efficiency of a racing car to paint it when the tires are flat and the engine is dead? Sure, it's important to improve the elegance of the instruction itself; smooth instruction helps motivation as well as ease of learning. But until the above items are attended to, improved elegance isn't likely to net you much gain in instructional success.

So work to make the course responsive to a real need before working to improve the elegance of the course materials. Work to provide students with a real reason to learn before working to improve the quality of your slides. Remember the Wacky Watchmaker who worked hard to reduce the number of parts needed for a wristwatch. When asked whether it worked, he replied, "Certainly not. But it doesn't work—*efficiently.*"

And keep in mind that Rome wasn't burned in a day. Make your changes one at a time. And then reward yourself each time you do so.

In Closing

Instruction is an act of humanity. It is an attempt to enrich the lives of others by expanding their ability to deal more successfully with the world in which they live. The measure of our success is the degree to which we can make our graduates employable, self-sufficient, and socially adept. There are few callings more personally rewarding or of greater importance to society than that of contributing to the success of others.

Useful Resources

1. Carlisle, K. E. *Analyzing Jobs and Tasks,* 1986. Educational Technology Publications, Inc. 140 Sylvan Avenue, Englewood Cliffs, NJ 07632.

2. Cram, D. D. "Professor T-Pop." *Performance and Instruction,* July, 1979; pp. 38–41.

3. Cram, D. D. "Advice to the Training-Lorn," *Performance and Instruction,* March, 1983; pp. 26–27.

4. Harless, J. H. "Guiding Performance with Job Aids," *Introduction to Performance Technology,* 1986, pp. 106–124.

5. Hoffman, M. "What to Leave Out When Time Is Short," *Performance and Instruction,* April, 1987.

6. Mager, R. F., and Pipe, P. *Analyzing Performance Problems,* Third Edition, 1997.

7. Mager, R. F., and Pipe, P. Performance Analysis Flowchart and Worksheets (24/pkg.), 1997.

8. Mager, R. F. *How to Turn Learners On . . . without turning them off,* Third Edition, 1997.

9. Mager, R. F. *Goal Analysis,* Third Edition, 1997.

10. Mager, R. F. *Measuring Instructional Results,* Third Edition, 1997.

11. Mager, R. F. *Preparing Instructional Objectives,* Third Edition, 1997.

12. Mager, R. F. *What Every Manager Should Know About Training,* 1992.

13. Mager, E. W. *Classroom Presentation Skills Workshop*, Third Edition, 1997.

14. Mager, R. F. *Applied CRI*, 1987.

15. Mager, R. F., and Pipe, P. *Criterion-Referenced Instruction: Practical Skills for Designing Instruction that Works*, 4th ed., 1994.

16. Mager, R. F. *Instructional Module Development*, 2nd ed., Revised 1996.

17. Mager, R. F. "No Self-Efficacy, No Performance," *Training Magazine*, Lakewood Publications, April, 1992.

18. Schrock, Sharon A., and Coscarelli, William C. C. *Criterion-Referenced Test Development*, 1996. ISBN: 0-9616690-22-0.

19. Tosti, D. T. "Feedback Systems," *Introduction to Performance Technology*, 1986; pp. 166–167.

20. Pipe, P. *Developing Performance Aids Workshop*, Peter Pipe Associates, 1981. Peter Pipe Associates, 962 Chehalis Drive, Sunnyvale, CA 94087.

Resources 6 through 16 are available from:

> The Center for Effective Performance, Inc.
> 4250 Perimeter Park South, Suite 131
> Atlanta, GA 30341   (770) 458-4080
>   (800) 558-4237

Resources 2, 3, 4, 5, and 19 are available from:

> International Society for Performance Improvement
> 1300 L Street NW, Suite 1250, Washington, DC 20005

Makenzie Mit Der Bookentesting

The house lights dimmed and the orchestra charged into the overture. Cymbals crashed, trombones trombled, and trumpets hootled. Violin bows flashed and bobbled in unison, as though locked together in a frenzy of musical calisthenics.

"That's a pretty enthusiastic overture," said the novice. "What's this opera about, anyway?"

"Well," responded the regular, "it's a tribute."

"Tribute? To what or whom?"

"To a clump of folks who were generous enough to help the hero test his book. The opera opens with the hero sitting at the typewriter, writing a book. He begins by singing and whining about how hard it is to write. It's a very sad aria."

"Sounds like a nut. What happens then?"

"His wife comes in . . . Lola Lollapalooza. She's a soprano played by Eileen Mager. She tells him about her day in the village. Then they sing a duet, with her trying to get him to let her see the book, and him subtly trying to get back to work."

At this point the first act ended and the smokers ran for the exits.

"What happens next?" asked the novice.

"The next act takes place after he's finished a first draft and is ready to try it out."

"Try it out?"

"Yes. Before he sends it to the publisher, he wants to know whether the book has the right content for its audience and whether it's as clear and useful as he can make it."

"Isn't he smart enough to answer that for himself?"

"Well," replied the seasoned one, "he's smart enough to know that his mind-reading skills aren't very good. So to make sure he's headed in a useful direction, he's asked someone to check it for continuity and completeness."

"Aha."

"Here he comes now. The first person to run his mind over the manuscript is Doctor Magic Whizzmore, played by Paul Whitmore."

Just then a dashing figure in flowing robes entered and began to sing in sonorous tones.

"Why is he carrying that box under his arm?"

"That's his computer. He always carries it. It's connected to his oblong medulla. Shhh. Listen as he tells the writer about his findings, about his reactions to the content. It's a very moving aria."

"Now what?"

The soprano had returned and repeated her aria entreating the writer to let her see his work. He bent down to tie his shoelace; while on his knees he begged the question.

"The suggested revisions have now been made and another tryout has been done, this time by the baritone in the purple knickers waving the golf club. This role is being consummately played by David Cram . . . he plays it often. He's singing about how he checked the manuscript for completeness and content, as well as for its integrity in the corporate training environment."

"Does he always carry that golf club?" queried the novice.

"He has to. It's attached to him. His doctor has told him that if he ever unscrews the golf club from his hand, his bottom will fall off."

"This seems like a long opera."

"They all do. The music covers the absence of plot, and the loud singing helps keep the audience awake. But we're nearing the climax. Look. Here come the Teepoppers."

"The what?"

"The Teepoppers. They represent the target audience of the book. They have a great deal of instructional experience, especially in the vocational and technical training environments. They're singing their recommendations. These roles are brilliantly played by Bob Miller and Jim Maxey. This is important stuff. Notice how closely the writer is paying attention and making notes."

"Wait a minnit. Here comes that soprano again. What does she want now?"

"Same thing. Wants to offer her help, but the husband keeps telling her he's saving her for the grand finale. Even so, she's good for his morale."

"How does it come out in the end?"

"Wait and see. Look. Another round of revision has been completed, and the writer has sent out copies for technical accuracy."

"I thought he just did that."

"That was to make sure the content would work for the audiences it is intended for. This check was to make sure that the procedures described are psychologically sound, accurately apply principles of learning, and won't unintentionally turn the readers off."

"Looks like a parade is starting."

"No. It's just that each of the people asked to check technical accuracy sings a recommendations solo in turn. Gives us a chance to see some colorful costumes as we listen to their wisdom."

"Who are playing these roles?"

"Those roles are incomparably played by Marianne

Hoffman, Bill Valen, Carol Valen, and Paul Whitmore."

At this point the soprano returned, the curtain came down on the second act, and the smokers ran for the exits.

"The last act opens with the chorus singing about the title check," confided the veteran. "The writer has asked a number of people to respond to several possible titles. They sing about their choices while the writer sings about the importance of making the title fit the intended user."

"I've just become glad they don't sing this stuff in English."

"If you will think about it, you will see that this is a very important part of the process. How often would you buy a steak that was called dead cow?"

"I see your point. Who are these people?"

"These roles are ably played by Al Wilson, Carol Valen, Lex Danson, John Pate, Skip Wolfe, Millar Farewell, Seth Leibler, Joyce Kelly, Verne Niner, Bill Valen, Alan Steffes, and Eileen Mager."

"The soprano finally got a whack at it?"

"Yes. And now she's into her big scene. She was saved for last, y'know. Loved ones can be the hardest critics, and he didn't want to take a chance on being demoralized before he finished. But she finally got to do her manuscript tryout and is now singing her recommendations."

"Long, isn't it?"

"But beautifully sung."

"Why is that lady in the red mask and black cape slashing at the manuscript?"

"That's the editor, played by Mary Kitzmiller. She's the heavy, acting out how she sliced words and punctured phrases to ready the manuscript for publication."

"Couldn't he write?"

"No matter how well he writes, there are always hundreds of changes that will make the product more readable, more literate, more interesting. Also gives editors a feeling of power."

Just then another group of colorfully-clad singers marched in.

"Now what? I thought it was over."

"Oh, these are the people who tested the new edition. Their chorus is an operatic version of 'Pick a Little, Talk a Little, Pick, Pick Pick.' It's very important and is being very well sung by David Cram, Ann Parkman, Seth Leibler, Lola Lollapalooza (Eileen Mager), John Gaylord, Dan Raymond, Marianne Hoffman, and Paul Whitmore.

"Quite a handsome group, wouldn't you say?"

"Look. Here's the grand finale. The writer has assembled all the contributors into his den . . ."

"Big den."

"Artistic license. He's describing their important contributions to the development of the book and is singing the praises of each in turn. He's imploring the audience to stand in awe at their assistance and to applaud their generosity until their hands turn red. Let's join in."

And so they did.

Index

Dr. Robert F. Mager has authored one of the most extensive and renowned collections of books and resources on issues of human performance in existence today. These books are considered to be *the* reference library for anyone serious about educating others and improving human performance. You'll find everything you need to learn how to:

- develop successful instruction,
- find realistic solutions to performance problems,
- measure the results of your instruction,
- generate positive attitudes in learners,
- and much more!

Order your copies today and get resources you'll use for a lifetime.

	Quantity	x Price=	Total
Measuring Instructional Results *How to determine whether your instructional results have been achieved*		x $19.95=	
Preparing Instructional Objectives *A critical tool in the development of effective instruction*		x $19.95=	
How to Turn Learners On... without turning them off *Ways to ignite interest in learning*		x $19.95=	
Analyzing Performance Problems *How to figure out why people aren't doing what they should be, and what to do about it*		x $19.95=	
Making Instruction Work *A step-by-step guide to designing and developing instruction that works*		x $19.95=	
Goal Analysis *How to clarify your goals so you can actually achieve them*		x $19.95=	
The How to Write a Book Book		x $17.95=	
Troubleshooting the Troubleshooting Course		x $17.95=	
What Every Manager Should Know About Training		x $17.95=	
Subtotal			
Shipping & Handling*			
GA residents add 5% sales tax to the subtotal plus shipping and handling			
Total Order			

* Please add $4.50 for the first book, plus $1.50 for each additional book. Please allow four weeks for delivery by UPS Ground Service.

Name _____

Phone_____Fax _____

Organization_____

Address_____

City_____ State _____ Zip_____

• My check or money order for $ _____is enclosed

Charge my • Visa • Mastercard • AmEx   Exp. Date _____

Card Number_____

Name on Card_____

Please send this form and your check, money order, or credit card number to:

CEP
P.O. Box 102462
Atlanta, GA 30368-2462

Call 1-800-558-4CEP for volume discount information.

Call for shipping charges on international orders.

For credit card orders, fax this order for faster delivery: (770) 458-9109